GOD'S WAY OUT OF DEPRESSION

ELLEL MINISTRIES
TRUTH AND FREEDOM SERIES

GOD'S WAY OUT OF DEPRESSION

DAVID CROSS

Sovereign World

Published by Sovereign World Ltd
Ellel Grange, Ellel Ministries, Bay Horse,
Lancaster, LA2 0HN
www.sovereignworld.com

ISBN: 978-1–85240-809-1

Cover design by Paul Stanier, Zaccmedia
Typeset by Graeme Andrew Envydesign Ltd.
Printed and bound in Great Britain by Bell and Bain Ltd, Glasgow

To Denise, my wife, my helper and my friend.

The journey of life would have lacked so much colour, adventure and fun without you beside me.

Contents

Thank You

My sincere thanks to Amy, Annie, Imogen, Derek, Iris, Deidre, James, Lilly, Peter, Lucy, Anthony and Hannah, for sharing a little of your lives for the purposes of this book. Your stories will continue to be an inspiration to everyone who is on a similar healing journey with Jesus.

Many thanks also to all those who have advised me on the content of this book, in particular Bayo, Beatriz, Grace and Julie. Your experience and wisdom have been so very helpful.

Introduction

If you're currently struggling with depression and you haven't got the energy just now to persevere through all the pages of this book, make a start by looking at chapter 5. It gives an outline of strategic steps for God's roadmap out of depression. Remember, with Him nothing is impossible! My prayer is that you will be encouraged through all the pages of this book and you will experience God's guidance on your journey of healing.

World-wide, depression is becoming a leading cause of illness. Around twenty percent of the population in the United Kingdom suffer some form of depression during their lives. In America, rates of suicide and depression among fifteen to twenty-five-year-olds have doubled in the past decade.

In response to statistics such as these, I want to declare a passionate belief that God has an answer, and this book will try to explore the issue, as far as possible, from His point of view. I will share a biblical perspective on secular diagnosis and treatment, and hopefully encourage you with real-life testimonies of people who have experienced God's healing from depression. Many Christians have sought Him for the root causes of this affliction and have followed His way of restoration into a place of genuine freedom.

Within the pages of this book you will meet twelve of these individuals who have experienced, beyond any doubt, God bringing radical healing in their lives from the bondage of major depression. Amy, Annie, Imogen, Derek, Iris, Deidre, James, Lilly, Peter, Lucy, Anthony and Hannah all have very different stories concerning the causes of their struggle with depression, and they have walked different journeys of restoration. However, each one has recognised that, in order to know true freedom, they have needed a spiritual transformation in their lives as well as healing of the mind. I have specifically called each of them *our friend*, firstly because I have known them personally, and secondly because their willingness to share something of their life-story with us in this book, has led me to see them as companions to every reader.

The content of this book is not intended, in any way, to undermine the valuable work of the medical profession in trying to alleviate the distress of this debilitating disorder. However, having spoken to a number of doctors, they are often the first to admit that determining the causes, and choosing the right treatment for depression, remain very challenging areas of medicine. The biology of depression remains largely a mystery. Most of the medication prescribed for this disorder is relatively safe, symptom management being the main goal, even though there might not be a full cure for the underlying causes.

There is an important point that I want to stress. In the Body of Christ, we have a unique opportunity, because of the authority and compassion of Jesus, to address the spiritual damage in a person's life, a vital aspect in healing from depression. This opportunity is not available to the secular therapist. Christian healing is the restoration of God's created order in a person's life, which He brings to us through our entering into real relationship with Him. It is not just the management of the disorder, however important that management might be in the short term. Jesus made a powerful promise to His followers:

> *John 10:10... The thief comes only to steal and kill and destroy; I came that that they may have life, and have it abundantly.*
>
> *NASB*

Let's take Jesus at His word.

CHAPTER 1

What is depression?

How it feels

"I burst into tears a lot. It felt out of my control. I felt extremely tired. I didn't appreciate people coming to see me because it took away my sleeping time. I felt surrounded by darkness. I had no energy for, nor interest in, anything or anyone. Nothing mattered. I went through the motions of life, but I wasn't really part of it. Hopelessness was uppermost. I actually wanted to be dead."

These were the words of *our friend Imogen* as she remembered how she felt when major depression unexpectedly gripped her in her thirties, during a very difficult time in her life as a young mother living in very cramped conditions. At the same time, her husband was being threatened with the loss of his job and she was coping with a seriously ill three-year-old child.

Imogen was then, and still is, an active Christian. At the time of her struggle with depression it seemed to her that God was playing nasty tricks, and she even became angry with Him because, as a Christian, she felt unable to take her own life. She couldn't understand why God was allowing these things to happen, when she was seeking to follow Him.

Then, quite unexpectedly, something happened during a family meal, a moment which started Imogen on the pathway of healing. God quite clearly spoke into her heart, "It's because of your mother!" We'll return to Imogen's story later in this chapter, and we'll see how this unexpected revelation began to expose the early root issues behind her painful bout of depression, which had been triggered by the difficult circumstances of her life at that time.

God knows every detail of our lives right from conception. He created us to live abundant lives in intimate relationship with Him, but sadly, the sinfulness of humankind has damaged all lives to one degree or another. We therefore experience traumatic and painful times which can have ongoing effects throughout our lives. The feelings of despair that Imogen experienced, when she was in the depths of depression, certainly cannot be described as abundant life and, in that dark place, it can be extremely hard to receive the love of God.

Such feelings are not God's intended order for our lives. Like any good parent, our Heavenly Father wants to restore us from those things that cause us distress. Depression will never stop God loving us, but He doesn't love the pain that we experience. His heart has always been to bring peace and healing, and Jesus declares this truth about God in some well-known words:

> *Matthew 11:28… "Come to Me, all who are weary and heavy-laden, and I will give you rest."*
>
> *NASB*

Depression is not a sign of stupidity or moral weakness

Depression is found in every age group and all levels of society, and very often in those whom we would regard as having strong characters. Many eminent historical figures have suffered from this painful condition, including Winston Churchill, Abraham Lincoln, Samuel Johnson and John Bunyan, although historically it was often called melancholy. Many individuals in the Bible suffered bouts of deep despair, for example Elijah (1 Kings 19:4) and even King David, someone described as being a man after God's own heart (1 Samuel 13:14). David suffered times of extreme despondency, brought about both through his own actions and through those of others, and he frequently cried out to the Lord for help.

> *Psalm 6:2-6… I am worn out, O Lord; have pity on me! Give me strength; I am completely exhausted and my whole being is deeply troubled. How long, O Lord, will you wait to help me? Come and save me, Lord; in your mercy rescue me from death… I am worn out with grief; every night my bed is damp from my weeping; my pillow soaked with tears.*
>
> *GNB*

> *Psalm 38:5-8… My wounds grow foul and fester because of my folly. I am bent over and greatly bowed down; I go mourning all day long. For my loins are filled with burning, and there is no soundness in my flesh. I am benumbed and badly crushed; I groan because of the agitation of my heart.*
>
> *NASB*

In Psalm 38, David gives a very full description of the bodily distress that he is experiencing from both the hostility of those around him and from his own sinful reactions. In this verse he uses a word translated as *benumbed.* He is saying that the place of despair that has overwhelmed him has sucked the very life out of his being. Where is this deep place within us that God intended to be a life-supporter but, in the midst of depression, is so unable to sustain us? In Proverbs a similar sense of helplessness is expressed, giving an important clue about the core issue.

> *Proverbs 18:14...The spirit of a man can endure his sickness, but as for a broken spirit who can bear it?*
>
> *NASB*

We will explore the reality of this significant place within us, the human spirit, later in the book.

Defining the problem

Someone recently described major depression in the following words: your entire world is seen only through the lens of sadness, hopelessness, mourning, loss, emptiness, grief, pain, anger, frustration, guilt and death. Unlike many other types of sickness, the diagnosis of depression is only possible through assessment of symptoms rather than through measurement of any quantifiable biology within the body.

Let's consider the sort of indicators that doctors look for in their assessment of a patient. Major or clinical depression will be diagnosed if the person has experienced, over at least a couple of weeks, one or two of the core symptoms plus a few more symptoms from anywhere on the full list below. If these symptoms are impairing their normal function, the severity may then be assessed by the number of indicators being experienced.

Core symptoms:

- Persistent absence of positive emotions
- Lack of interest / motivation in previously enjoyed activities
- Altered appetite / eating patterns
- Agitation, anxiety, panic attacks
- Persistent deep fatigue, loss of energy
- Sense of worthlessness and failure
- Low self-confidence
- Hopelessness
- Loss of outward affection and sex-drive

Other common symptoms:

- Mental confusion / indecision
- Suicidal thoughts, preoccupation with death
- Altered sleep patterns
- Persistent guilty feelings
- Personality change
- Emotional numbness
- Irritability
- Desire to cut off from people, to withdraw
- Loss of concentration
- Reduced walking speed and arm swing
- Repeated patterns of negative thinking

- Neglect in personal appearance
- Nightmares, such as being overwhelmed by the dark
- Uncontrollable weeping
- Headaches, palpitations

Patients may initially present with the physical symptoms of headaches or a sleep disorder, for example, finding it difficult to admit that they are really struggling with depression. They might feel that depression is not a real disease, or they might be worried that the doctor will immediately refer them to a psychiatrist. It is important that we all get more used to talking about this painful disorder in a way that does not stigmatise the people who are suffering.

Another point to recognise is that by the time people with depression get to the doctor, some will have been trying to get through with their own coping mechanisms which might be alcohol, drugs, disordered eating patterns or isolation. Alcohol, for example, will actually make depression worse and often prevents the effectiveness of antidepressant medication. Very occasionally, people might use a diagnosis of depression to justify ungodly lifestyle choices which they see as necessary to cope with their mental distress. Depression, although very painful, should never be allowed to place someone beyond well-meaning confrontation of their damaging choices, provided that this challenge is truly done with loving kindness and sensitivity.

The limitations of secular treatment

We can be truly grateful to God for the wisdom, skill and perseverance of the medical profession in seeking to alleviate the devastating symptoms of depression. However, we need to face the reality that without an intervention from Jesus in regard to the spiritual issues surrounding depression, secular treatment will inevitably have limitations.

Let me describe some of the experiences of *our friend Lilly*, during the time she was seeking help for depression, which she knew was mainly rooted in past trauma within her marriage. After seeking help from her doctor, and receiving a prescription of antidepressants, Lilly was asked to fill in a questionnaire about her appetite, sleep patterns and suicidal thoughts. As a result of her answers she was told that her condition was too serious for standard counselling, so she agreed to psychiatric appointments at a local clinic.

Despite experiencing panic attacks before the first appointment, she found the consultant psychiatrist to be gentle and helpful. However, when she arrived for the next appointment the following week, she was told that the consultant she had seen before was not available. Although the staff at the clinic were very well-meaning, there were further cancellations over the following weeks, due to the consultant being on sick leave. Sadly, these unexpected changes were enough to send Lilly into a spiral of anxiety and hopelessness, but this was not the end of her story. In the midst of this increasingly desperate situation, God stepped in.

On the way home from a cancelled appointment, Lilly heard the Lord say the words *beauty for ashes*, and in a remarkable way He led her to a Christian ministry of that name where she began, for the first time, to feel hope that God had an answer. Afterwards, she went to a restoration week at the Ellel Ministries' centre of Glyndley Manor and this started a remarkable pathway of God's healing from the depression.

Here are her words:

> "I went with trepidation and fear. I was still on sleeping tablets, antidepressants and diazepam to help with the panic attacks. Many people there [at Glyndley Manor] were in the same place as me and suffering through different reasons. You didn't have to be all together to be accepted! After just one day, God dramatically touched my life with new joy, overwhelming joy. I thought I was there to be healed from a life of abuse, but God knew that what I needed right then, to help me get back on my feet, was joy. Everyone said, when I got home that they didn't recognise me! It was just the start of the healing journey but the change in me was incredible."

Lilly's story reminds us that however well-intentioned and necessary secular treatment may be, to provide short-term relief from depression, the medical profession is not well placed to meet the deep heart-cry for restoration of the human spirit. God had pointed Lilly to a key verse in scripture:

> *Isaiah 61:3a... [He has sent me] to bestow on them a crown of beauty instead of ashes, the oil of gladness instead of mourning, and a garment of praise instead of a spirit of despair.*
>
> *NIV*

The symptoms of depression listed earlier, particularly those feelings of low self-confidence, hopelessness and worthlessness, point to damage not just in the mind but in the human spirit. This is a deep part of our being which holds the key to our sense of identity and, for some, can be filled with despair. However, this is a place where God can truly restore confidence in our identity, our destiny and our value. We shall later explore this inner place of the human spirit but, for now, here's the continuation of Imogen's story which started this chapter.

God revealed unexpected roots to Imogen

Whilst struggling with a serious bout of depression *our friend Imogen* unexpectedly heard God speak into her heart, "It's because of your mother." This was a surprise to her as she had considered herself to have had a good relationship with her mother but, when she recalled what she'd been told about her childhood, she began to recognise that there had been some serious issues.

The first two years of Imogen's life had been spent in the house of her mother's mother, in a very negative atmosphere because of this grandmother's disapproval of Imogen's father. Desperate to have a well-behaved and quiet baby in this difficult environment, Imogen's mother followed, to the letter, strict rules listed in a book about caring for babies. These rules included, for example, no night-time feeds as soon as mother and baby came home from hospital.

This resulted in a very harsh regime of frequent isolation for Imogen and she apparently became resigned to the fact that it wasn't worth asking for the comfort that she craved. Her mother told her many years later that, as a tiny baby, Imogen had just "gone quiet" and stopped asking for food and attention.

As she brought these issues to the Lord, Imogen recognised profound feelings of being unwelcome and of having no assurance of being loved. God's healing process was a very new concept for her, but step by step she forgave her mother, her grandmother and even the author of the book on caring for babies. God showed Imogen's husband a way for her to pray regularly, based on Ezekiel 47. It was about walking each day more deeply into the water of life and, after a few months, there came a day when God spoke again into her heart and told her that it was done, and that she didn't have to pray like that anymore.

Imogen acknowledges that she has since lived through further emotional ups and downs, but she has never again gone down into the same very dark place.

> She commented recently, when recording her journey of healing, "I now understand much more clearly that this healing was happening not so much in my mind but in my human spirit."

This reference to her human spirit will be very important for us to explore later in the book.

Terms and medical conditions associated with depression

Over many years the different forms of depression have been given names by the medical profession to help with determining the appropriate treatment. There are also associated disorders that very often exhibit similar symptoms to major depression. I will briefly mention a number of these because it has become clear in prayer ministry that despite the different labels, there can often be similar causes. Negative experiences in childhood that have deeply affected a person seem to be a very common root issue. This list is not intended to be exhaustive, nor is it a full description of the particular labels that are used; it is simply meant to be an aid in our exploration of God's answer to depression.

- Reactive depression: bouts of depression that appear to be the consequence of current difficult life situations.
- Endogenous depression: bouts of depression with no clear current causes, potentially coming from unresolved inner issues from the past.
- Unipolar depression: the kind of depression where a person remains in a place of persistent despair for a significant period. This is the main area being considered within the pages of this book, and it will be referred to as clinical or major depression.
- Bipolar disorder: previously referred to as manic depression, this kind of depression exhibits marked changes moving between extremes of despair and overactivity.
- Cyclothymia: a milder form of bipolar disorder.
- Post-natal depression: usually a short-lived form of depression following the huge chemical and emotional changes to the body during the momentous experience of childbirth. It can, however, be a trigger into longer term depression related to unresolved issues from the past.
- Seasonal affective disorder (SAD): this is not just winter blues but a type of major depressive disorder that

appears to be linked with certain times of the year, such as the darker days of winter.

- Obsessive compulsive disorder: an addictive type of behaviour responding to irrational, demanding and anxious thought patterns.
- Eating disorders: compulsive and dysfunctional eating patterns related to personal image and control mechanisms.
- Self-harming: a choice to inflict physical pain or damage to the body, very often in an attempt to relieve inner distress and sometimes guilt.
- Personality disorder: a wide-ranging term for mental and identity issues which are causing the patient a significant measure of distress when compared with the average person.
- Paranoia: an irrational fear of persecution.
- Schizophrenia: a long-term mental disorder, which can include hallucinations, muddled thinking and behavioural swings, characterised by a loss of connection with reality in some areas.
- Burnout: a crisis point of collapse of inner reserves, when the output of physical and emotional energy appears to exceed the input.

This list can seem a bit overwhelming but let me record again here the verse that was written in the introduction to this book, because there is very good news! Jesus has stepped into this world as the answer to all the robbery of human peace and destiny, the solution to the theft that is promoted by the evil one.

John 10:10... The thief comes only to steal and kill and destroy; I came that they may have life, and have it abundantly.

NASB

Key points from this chapter

- Major depression is experienced during their lifetime by more the 250 million people worldwide, affecting individuals in many different ways. The medical profession seeks to categorise types of depression in order to provide better descriptions of the actual effects on an individual, and to help provide appropriate treatment.

- Nobody chooses to suffer the distress of depression, and it's not a sign of weakness or moral failing. In fact, it seems very often to be associated with people who might be described as having a strong character.

- Events that trigger a bout of depression are rarely the root cause of the problem. Very often, it seems that recognition of unresolved trauma from the past, and the environment in which a person has grown up, can be a key to the healing journey.

- We thank God for the medical profession and all that is done to help those suffering. However, for followers of Jesus, there is an opportunity to explore the spiritual aspects of this disorder and to seek a deeper restoration and freedom.

- The recognised symptoms of depression, such as a sense

of worthlessness, clearly point beyond just a mood disorder but rather to damage deep within a person's identity, in our precious human spirit.

CHAPTER 2

Secular and Christian responses to depression

Causes of depression

From a secular and medical point of view, the exact causes of depression are unclear. Various factors are recognised as being responsible for altering the brain's neural networks and disrupting hormone levels. Personality and gender appear to affect susceptibility, with women twice as prone to major depression as men, whereas bipolar depression, which is thought to be largely genetic in origin and triggered by stress, seems to affect both genders to the same degree. Women are four times more prone to SAD than men, most often between the ages of eighteen and thirty. All depression tends to become less common as people age, but there remains a problem that older people are less likely to seek help for mental health issues. It is increasingly recognised that there are multiple factors that can contribute to the disorder, including genetic predisposition, social conditions, the side effects of other medical issues and, not least, the consequence of earlier life traumas. Some researchers have explored the relevance of sleep patterns and dreaming, because our sleeping time is believed to be valuable in processing unresolved life-issues. For depressed people, that important part of the sleeping time seems to be in overload because of the level of unresolved issues that require subconscious rumination. This can lead to insufficient rest time in sleep and even more distress to the body.

Our main purpose in this book is to focus on the likely spiritual issues that lie at the root of depression, but we do need to acknowledge the physical issues that so clearly surround this disorder. Family and friends should watch out for the previously listed indicators of depression in their loved ones, especially when these symptoms last more than a couple of weeks. This is particularly important with the elderly, because physical illness is very often associated with mental health issues in older adults.

Depression is sometimes linked to particular medical conditions

Besides the emotional and spiritual roots of major depression, there are a number of medical conditions that are known to sometimes be the cause of bouts of depression in people's lives, or at least be a trigger to underlying susceptibility. Studies have shown that people who have experienced heart disease, including heart failure or a heart attack, are more likely to develop depression than those who have not. In addition, the prescribed medication for heart conditions, as indeed for a number of other diseases, may itself have the side-effect of triggering depression.

When someone has experienced a life-threatening event such as a heart attack, it's very likely that their thoughts are going to turn more to the issue of their mortality, but for some this can become a consuming issue. It's important for those who have suffered a heart event to take particular care of themselves with regard to diet, sleep, relaxation and avoiding demanding commitments. It's also a good opportunity to seek a deeper and more secure relationship with God, learning to trust Him in the midst of medical vulnerability. Incidentally, as well as being a possible cause, heart disease can also be a consequence for those suffering with depression. It can significantly raise a person's risk, probably due to the increased stress in the body that accompanies depression.

Other conditions that are known to sometimes be a contributory cause or trigger for depression include an under-active thyroid, dementia, Parkinson's disease, Lyme disease, polymyalgia rheumatica, head injury, recovery from operations, severe vitamin and mineral deficiency, hormonal imbalance, diabetes, cancer and the effects of prescribed and recreational drugs. High alcohol consumption is one of the most potent and common physical causes of depression.

There can be some surprising causes

Our friend Derek remembers his first experience of overwhelming depression. Unusually, it lasted for only for a few days. He was working in a veterinary practice around farms in Cornwall and woke one day to find himself struggling with a deep sense of despair. There developed strong suicidal thoughts and a sense of profound darkness in his life. Then almost as suddenly as it had begun, Derek woke a few days later to a feeling of lightness which increased during the day to a point of joy and relief.

The mystery of what had triggered these sudden symptoms became apparent a few weeks later. Seeking medical help for something completely different, Derek's doctor advised him that he had a very high level of brucellosis bacteria in his body, apparently picked up from his work among infected cattle on the farms. The symptoms of brucellosis infection in human beings is known to include deep depression, sometimes of a repetitive nature. Thankfully for Derek the problem never came back.

Derek's experience reminds us that depression can be the consequence of specific medical issues in the body. However, the complex interaction of the human body, soul and spirit remains something that only God fully understands, and it is very worthwhile to come to Him for revelation of how best to pray. We will hear in chapter 5 of this book how Derek suffered a much longer period of depression later in his life, triggered this time by an intensely stressful work situation. As God took him through a process of healing from a very unpleasant depressive experience, Derek realised that there were significant roots from his childhood, especially in the ways he had tried to deal with inner distress.

Medical management of depression

Even without medication or therapy, the majority of people overcome the symptoms of major depression within six months, although spontaneous recovery from bipolar disorder is far less likely without treatment. Recovery happens much more quickly with help, and some form of treatment is particularly important if the person is struggling with suicidal urges. Antidepressants can save lives. Even if recovery from depression takes place without medication or therapy, the question will remain as to whether the underlying causes of the depression have been resolved. Clearly the ideal outcome is to remove the core vulnerability rather than just manage or survive the symptoms.

Medical help through the prescribing of antidepressants or the provision of talking therapies will be, for many sufferers, an important step in managing the extreme symptoms of this painful disorder. Sadly, some people avoid seeking treatment for fear of being judged, while others feel ashamed at having to resort to medical intervention. This can be particularly true for Christians who may think that they are letting God down by needing secular help for an apparent mood disorder, when they feel that they should be full of the joy of the Lord!

The social stigma associated with depression has certainly lessened over the last few decades, but it's still easier for many people to admit to difficulties caused by physical disorders such as arthritis, rather than by depression. Physical illness is perhaps more easily understood by friends and family than a mental disorder. Ill-informed acquaintances might give the impression that they think the sufferer should just *snap out of it*! The truth is that for people struggling with major depression, they can't just turn off the symptoms nor *pull themselves together*. They need help.

I need to be very clear in regard to medical treatment: we all thank God that He has blessed the world with ever-improving medical ability which can alleviate suffering, by managing the symptoms of so many human disorders. When someone is walking with God on a journey towards full healing from depression, it's very important not to dismiss the probable need for secular medical help along the way, at least for a while. More than three-quarters of those treated for depression show improvement in their symptoms within a few weeks of beginning medication or psychotherapy. Studies have confirmed that many of the commonly prescribed antidepressant drugs are effective in managing moderate to severe depression. However, the level of effectiveness can vary widely, depending on the patient. Christians taking medication should certainly not be made to feel fearful or embarrassed but should be encouraged to seek God's way out of the problem. This can be alongside symptom management, through the use of anti-depressants, if these are needed.

Let's look at the two main areas of treatment offered by the medical profession to those diagnosed with major depression: talk-based therapies and antidepressant medication.

Secular talk-based therapies

A vital aspect of the journey out of depression is the need for the sufferer to be truly heard. Behind depression there will probably be a series of negative life experiences, with resulting beliefs, attitudes, thought patterns, emotions, decisions and behaviours. There are apparently more than four hundred schools of psychotherapy, each with a different emphasis on which part of that pathway from belief to behaviour most needs to be tackled in order to bring relief.

Approaches such as cognitive behavioural therapy (CBT) and supportive psychotherapy seek to establish more positive feelings and behaviours to counteract the depression. It's worth recording here that *our friend Derek* found CBT very helpful on his journey of healing. He was given a workbook and through a process of recording his responses to the issues of each day, he was able to counter the habitual negative ways of thinking which had reinforced the disorder. For Derek, it provided a useful addition to the way that God was leading and healing him, although he did have to give very clear boundaries to the therapist not to stray into techniques founded in Buddhist beliefs.

Psychodynamic therapy or psychoanalysis looks with more detail at the way past events may be driving the depression, but there is no attempt to consider the need for a spiritual resolution to those issues, from a Christian viewpoint. Many therapists will encourage clients to adopt a wider perspective, using words like *reframing*, helping them to recognise the positive aspects of their lives rather than just focusing on the negative. The therapists are well aware that self-pronouncements by the clients, such as *nothing will ever work for me*, need to be challenged.

Some schools of therapy specifically promote the view that depressed people are essentially caught up in exaggerated negative thoughts because there are deep and unmet emotional needs. They believe that this problem is best resolved by reviving the natural, but disabled, human resources within us. However, there is no awareness of the biblical truth of the fallen condition of humans, and the fact that this fundamentally affects our inner needs. As followers of Jesus, we recognise that such deprivation can only be fully resolved in a relationship with the One who created us, and in the deep sense of belonging that He intends for each of us within His family.

Other approaches encourage a positive use of imagination to process past and future life options. Out-of-body personal observation and other dissociative techniques are also used to apparently 'take the emotional power' out of past traumas. But the roots of depression are not truly resolved by these techniques, they are just made distant by the different methods of disconnection. Spiritually, this becomes problematic because any aspect of our lives that is left in the dark through dissociation can be destructive to our well-being, and even be an opportunity for spiritual oppression.

Antidepressant medication

Depression is not primarily a biological disorder but, whatever the root causes, it certainly affects the biology or chemistry of the body, not least in the brain.

Four times as many antidepressants are being consumed in the UK than twenty years ago, with currently around 70 million prescriptions each year in England alone. The most commonly prescribed antidepressants are called Selective Serotonin Reuptake Inhibitors (SSRIs), or Serotonin and Noradrenaline Reuptake Inhibitors (SNRIs). These antidepressants are given with the intention of balancing the levels of the neurotransmitters (serotonin and noradrenaline), which are chemicals involved in communication between neurons in the brain. Higher levels of these chemicals typically correspond with lower levels of depression.

The prescribed drugs are designed to counteract the chemical imbalances in the brain that are associated with depression. Any such chemical imbalance is a consequence and contributor to depression but is not its foundational cause. Whilst often very necessary, prescribed medication may have the effect of masking underlying issues and should not be seen as the easy way out by the medical profession or by the depressed person. Instead, they should be regarded as a temporary and important support on the journey of restoration.

Patience is important when taking antidepressants. It can take two weeks to start noticing any effect, and four to six weeks for the build-up of the medication to be most beneficial for the patient. Most people will need to remain on these drugs for at least six weeks, and often for several months. About one third of those taking antidepressants experience significant help, about one third a degree of help, and about one third experience no appreciable relief. On the other hand, the conventional medication for bipolar disorder, which is the chemical element lithium, has been found to be effective for almost all sufferers.

As with all medication, there will be a risk of unwanted side-effects from antidepressants, such as weight gain, headaches, nausea and diarrhoea. It may be necessary to try several types of medication to find the one that is well tolerated and effective for each individual. Withdrawal symptoms, when stopping antidepressants, can be serious for some users, even if the medication is not regarded as addictive. If this is the case, it can be helpful to switch to a different medication that is easier to stop taking, when this is medically advised.

Particularly with adolescents, there is a small increased risk of suicidal thoughts or behaviour for some people taking SSRIs, so follow-up sessions with the doctor are very important in the first few weeks of taking an antidepressant. When the time is right, people can and do successfully come off antidepressants, but it should always be under the guidance of a doctor, even if there is an awareness of God's healing taking place. Even Jesus told some of the people that

He restored to get their healing confirmed by those carrying the necessary authority.

> *Matthew 8:4b… Go, show yourself to the priest and present the offering that Moses commanded, as a testimony to them.*
> NASB

Facing the giant of suicide.

An increasing number of young people in their teen years, now probably as many as one in five, have seriously considered suicide. Low self-worth, in a world that is so very image-conscious, is deeply affecting countless lives. The potential of suicide is always a frightening thought for family and friends who are coming alongside those with depression. However, it needs to be openly faced whenever there is an indication that it is a significant thought in the mind of the sufferer. Here's a comment from someone who has walked through this issue. It might help dispel some of the fears for those trying to help:

> "When I was at my most unwell, only one friend dared to talk to me about suicide. She listened. She didn't judge. She let me voice my terrifying thoughts. It didn't make me more likely to kill myself. It didn't put ideas in my head. It made me feel better."

Suicidal thoughts often represent a desire to escape the overwhelming feelings of despair and, when someone talks of ways of committing suicide, it can be an indicator of real intent. As a carer or family member, it will be important to seek professional help in managing any crisis of this kind, and it's vital to be able to share the responsibility for the one who is struggling. At the same time, from a Christian point of view, the best antidote for the one thinking about suicide is for them to know, deep in their hearts, that God truly understands the struggles and that He sees them as having immeasurable worth. I read an article recently by a Christian Iranian lady describing her restoration from intense suicidal thoughts, which resulted in several attempts to take her own life. She said:

> "Forgive those who harmed you, or made you feel unloved or worthless. Forgive, because the act of forgiveness is the greatest prescription for the world."

We shall, of course, be exploring more of God's answer to these painful issues as we progress through the pages of this book.

Electroconvulsive therapy

Before I discuss electro-convulsive therapy (ECT), I will just clarify that another treatment, Magnetic Stimulation Therapy (or Transcranial Magnetic Stimulation), is not the same as ECT. It uses electromagnetism with the intention of stimulating nerve cells in the brain associated with mood. Although the biology for this is not fully understood, there has been of some benefit with certain patients, but there can also be a small risk of side effects such as brain seizures.

ECT appears to be effective for a significant percentage of patients suffering from severe depression, particularly when symptoms have become unmanageable by other therapies or medication. It is performed under general anaesthetic and works quickly by inducing a seizure in the brain, similar to the 'grand mal' episode of epilepsy. Typically, there will be eight to twelve sessions, over three to four weeks. The medical profession admits that they do not understand why the seizure improves the underlying psychiatric disorder but suspect that the brain's way of shutting off the seizure somehow brings the improvement. Electrodes are placed over one or both sides of the head to provide an electric shock, although far less electricity is used in ECT today than in the past. If the electrode is placed only over the right side this reduces the risk of cognitive side-effects, such as memory loss.

From a biblical perspective, and from the experience of prayer ministry, this electrical shock treatment appears to cause a fracture in the soul and spirit disconnecting the person today from the distress and despair of the past, which is trapped inside. Although there is often instant relief through ECT, the symptoms of depression tend to reappear after a period of time, but this therapy has been used widely in critical situations, particularly where someone's life is in danger from suicidal tendencies. Those advocating the procedure are, of course, very well-meaning but the inner fracture caused is not consistent with God's created order for the wholeness of a person's life. Therefore, it may well be important, at some stage during prayer ministry, to ask Him to repair the inner places that have been broken by this treatment.

> *Psalm 34:18... The Lord is close to the broken-hearted and saves those who are crushed in spirit.*
>
> *NIV*

Let me describe the experiences of *our friend Annie*. At the age of twenty-one, she was told that she needed to be hospitalised in a psychiatric unit, having been diagnosed with anorexia nervosa and endogenous depression (i.e. depression with no clear current causes). For her family, this was a cause of considerable shame, so she was told to neither phone nor post a letter lest the neighbours found out. She was advised that she needed ECT, as she had not responded to medication and, despite considerable personal anguish, she signed the necessary form permitting the treatment.

For Annie the immediate result, on waking up after the first session, was complete memory loss, needing the girl in the next bed to explain to her what had happened and where she was. However, she quickly felt much better and even euphoric because the inner torment had disappeared. The ECT continued for six weeks with two sessions each week, but the euphoria did not last long and the side-effects of memory loss and lethargy became hard to bear. The deep depression returned just as intensely as before and Annie recalls that, at this point, she just wanted to die.

After a further nine weeks of treatment, she felt that she had had enough and refused further ECT. Annie recalls that it was in the midst of this difficult choice about the treatment that she recognised that she needed to regain a sense of personhood and make clear decisions for her life.

> The doctors did not respond well to her stand, informing her that she would never be well again and would always need treatment. From somewhere deep within, Annie was able to say to them that only God could and would heal her.

It was not long after this, as the depression was once again getting worse, that she was invited to a Christian meeting where the healing power of Jesus was both taught and demonstrated. Here at last was the hope she had longed for, and for a number of years, though not fully healed, she did not need secular psychiatric help. She was able to find a level of stability, regularly sharing in the Word of God and in prayers with, what she described as, "authentic Christian believers".

Then Annie found an opportunity to start looking at the root issues behind the symptoms of depression and, after several times of prayer ministry, she knew that she was at last on the road to deeper healing. God began to reveal various experiences from the past where He brought healing, and she recognised the need to be less passive, making mature, godly choices in how to cope with the hurts that others had caused. She realises now that she has become much quicker to forgive both others and herself, and quicker to bring her pain to the Cross rather than adopting the old lifestyle of dissociation from pain.

Something that was also very significant for Annie was that God showed her that the ECT, although well-intentioned, had traumatised the whole of her being, including her human spirit. During a particular time of prayer ministry, God brought a clear awareness that even though she had been physically unconscious during the treatment sessions, her spirit had registered a flippant attitude among the doctors and nurses.

When she forgave them and asked the Lord to release her from the damaging brokenness of the shock and trauma in the sessions of ECT, Annie experienced an extraordinary and very powerful step of freedom.

Today, Annie says that she is still on the journey of healing, but it gets easier with every step. She leads a normal life, with a true joy, no longer suffering the destructive depression of the past, and she no longer needs to take any medication for the condition. Her sleep has returned after years of insomnia and, best of all, she has a much more intimate relationship with Jesus.

Recent medical research linking depression with dysfunction in the immune system [(a)]

Our immune system is an amazing God-designed barrier between our bodies and some of the biological and the physical threats that come from the world around us, for example from injury or infection. The immune system is an essential and complex part of our created being, standing between us and certain death from harmful bacteria and viruses. When the body detects such a threat, specific cells are attracted to the relevant location, for example in the intestinal tract (a very significant part of the immune system), to fight the perceived attack. This accumulation of cells causes inflammation, sometimes recognisable as red and swollen areas in the body. The brain and the body interact in producing and sharing the chemicals that cause this necessary inflammation.

Certain types of arthritis, which cause inflammation in the joints of the body, are linked to dysfunction of the immune

(a) Danese A. Moffit TE, Pariante CM, Ambler A, Poulton R, Caspi A. *Elevated inflammation levels in depressed adults with a history of childhood maltreatment.* Arch Gen Psychiatry. 2008;65:409-415

system. Some years ago, it was found that, when patients were given anti-inflammatory drugs to relieve the symptoms of arthritis, the medication seemed to be having a positive effect on a number of people who were also suffering from depression. When everything within us is functioning normally, the ebb and flow of inflammation is a healthy reaction to the day-to-day challenges to the body, but when the inflammation doesn't go away, this indicates something wrong within the immune system. Factors associated with persistent inflammation include disease, alcohol or drug use, loss of sleep, stressful situations and, notably for our investigations, childhood maltreatment and trauma.

The medical profession is not saying that depression is an inflammatory disorder, but immunological processes appear to play a pivotal role in some psychiatric disorders, including depression. There is strong evidence that persistent, perhaps low-grade inflammation, resulting from unresolved trauma in the past, does seem to be echoed in disrupted brain activity, and this affects the functioning of neurotransmitters such as serotonin. The problem may well be self-perpetuating in that depression and sleep disorder also increase inflammation in the body. This has resulted in the exploration of new treatment based on anti-inflammatory drugs rather than on the traditional SSRI antidepressants, particularly when, for some people, these antidepressants fail to be effective.

From a spiritual perspective we are getting yet more evidence that the physical symptoms of depression are very often the result of our body chemistry reflecting much deeper unresolved issues. These are likely to be emotional and spiritual trauma, together with beliefs and behaviours that have been developed in order to cope with the painful realities of life. When sinful choices are addressed and God is given the opportunity to repair that deeper damage, it is likely that the functioning of the immune system can come back into Godly order. Then the body will no longer be trying to fight the threats of the past, but instead can be restored to come in line with the heart change of 'a song of praise instead of sorrow' (Isaiah 61:3, GNB).

The roots of depression from a Christian perspective

Followers of Jesus have an advantage in comparison with all secular understanding and treatments associated with depression. Beyond all the valuable research that has taken place, beyond all the effective management of this widespread disorder through drugs and therapies, beyond the precious help of countless medical practitioners, Christians know the One who has all knowledge. God alone knows every distressing moment of our lives and the whole truth of how that distress has affected our body, soul and spirit.

He is also the One who is able to restore. He is the One who can heal damaged lives far beyond anything possible through just human intervention. The reality of the spiritual realm is not seen as relevant in most of mainstream treatment for depression, and yet this realm is at the core of all human disorder in this troubled world. We will be considering the roots of depression, not least disorder in the human spirit, in much more detail throughout the remainder of this book. In anticipation of that, let me summarise the key areas of spiritual damage that may well be at the root, for those struggling with major depression:

- Damage caused by inadequate parental covering. This can be from the moment of conception, particularly through insufficient protection and affirmation from our earthly father.
- Damage caused by specific incidents of trauma, such as abuse, loss and accidents. Unresolved issues of loss and abandonment seem to be commonly linked to depression.
- Damage caused by the ungodly spiritual ties that have developed in controlling relationships throughout our lives.
- Damage caused by personal involvement in false religion or the occult.
- Damage caused by personal sin within our beliefs, behaviours and lifestyle, such as passivity or abdication of personal responsibility.
- Damage caused by the effect of spiritual inheritance, where there has been generational iniquity distorting our lives and often predisposing us to disorders which are related to the wrongful lifestyles of our ancestors.

The good news is that, once we recognise the truth of what has happened in our lives, the healing heart of Jesus is sufficient for the repair of all this damage, and the power of the Holy Spirit is sufficient to give us victory in any sinful areas. We need only come to Him in forgiveness of others and receive His forgiveness and cleansing for ourselves.

God understands it all: sins, wounds and demons

It's not unusual, even in secular conversations, to hear people refer to their demons when talking about those parts of their lives that have felt particularly dark and troubling, not least in regard to the experiences of depression. For followers of Jesus, we need to look more carefully at this possible involvement of the powers of darkness.

The inner healing ministry of Jesus in our lives can be summarised as the resolution of sins, wounds and demons. However, we need discernment in order to know which we are dealing with at any given time, and then we need God's understanding of how to resolve each one of these issues. For example, it's neither necessary nor helpful to repent of being wounded! In short, sins need our repentance and God's forgiveness, wounds need our forgiveness of others, followed by God's repair, and demons need removal.

It's likely that the journey of finding freedom from depression will involve all three although, when first hearing this statement, it can seem a bit hard to take in. We need to be very careful neither to conclude that *it's all my fault*, nor conversely to assume that the causes of depression *can never include my being at fault*. Jesus made it very clear, as He walked on this earth, that the healing of wounded people is a significant aspect of what it means to be part of His Kingdom. However, as we read in a previous chapter, He never shied away from confronting people with sin issues in their lives when these were a contributory factor in their disorder.

> *John 5:14... Afterward Jesus found him in the temple and said to him, "Behold, you have become well; do not sin anymore, so that nothing worse happens to you."*
>
> *NASB*

There is no condemnation in these words of Jesus, just a compassionate warning of the reality of how sin can affect our lives. Jesus was also very ready to tackle the powers of darkness when necessary, while at the same time showing unbounded love for the individual in distress from enemy activity.

> *Luke 13:16... "And this woman, a daughter of Abraham as she is, whom Satan has bound for eighteen long years, should she not have been released from this bond on the Sabbath day?"*
>
> *NASB*

The reality of a prowling lion

Many people suffering from depression are driven to despair, self-rejection and self-harm, often in the form of suicidal thoughts. These characteristics are typical of the nature of the ruler of this world, whom Jesus describes as one who lies, steals, destroys and murders (John 8:44, John 10:10)

When we explore the causes of this disorder it is significant that there often seems to be spiritual oppression accompanying or even driving the emotional depression. The Bible tells us that the enemy prowls around our lives looking for the opportunity to get a grip on us (1 Peter 5:8). Such opportunity is given through our negligence, through deliberate sin or through the sin of those who carry a measure of responsibility for our well-being. It is as if the enemy is waiting to be given a licence to get into the driving seat of our lives and steer us away from all that God wants for us in our God-ordained identity as His children. We need to be on the alert and wise to the enemy's tricks:

> *2 Corinthians 2:11… In order that Satan might not outwit us. For we are not unaware of his schemes.*
>
> *NIV*

Occasionally, there can be an extreme assault of demonic intrusion in someone's life, driving the feelings of despair. We see this in the story of the man living in the territory of Gerasa, compelled to live in a place of death, and horribly driven to self-harm.

> *Mark 5:5… Day and night he wandered among the tombs and through the hills, screaming and cutting himself with stones.*
>
> *GNB*

Jesus stepped into the life of this desperate individual and dealt with the deep inner wounding and the accompanying torment from the powers of darkness. There is no disorder in the life of human beings that is beyond His reach and His authority. The ability of Jesus to restore lives was, and still is, literally awesome.

> *Mark 5:15… And when they [the people] came to Jesus, they saw the man who used to have the mob of demons in him. He was sitting there, clothed and in his right mind; and they were all afraid.*
>
> *GNB*

Of course, very few people are going to experience anything like this level of spiritual oppression, but it's important to be alert to the reality of the opportunities that we can give to the one that Jesus calls the ruler of the world.

Demonic oppression can come from involvement in the occult or in false religion such as Freemasonry. When we willingly give control to the enemy this can be hugely defiling to our human spirit. It allows us to be driven by powers of darkness that are intent on promoting the very opposite of the abundant life promised to us by Jesus, separating us from our true identity in Christ.

It isn't just activities such as the occult (which we will further consider later) that open the door to this prowling lion. We can unwittingly give licence to the enemy when we suppress strong feelings such as anger that results from injustice we have experienced. God designed us to express our emotions and passions at the time of their appearance, not to bury them. We may have been tempted to suppress them because of how other people might respond.

The Word of God tells us clearly that such suppression can give the powers of darkness a foothold in our lives, holding onto this place of spiritual darkness and using it against us. Interestingly, many writers on the issues surrounding depression have noticed a link with buried anger.

> *Ephesians 4:26-27... "In your anger do not sin": Do not let the sun go down while you are still angry, and do not give the devil a foothold.*
>
> *NIV*

Preparing the way for God's intervention

John the Baptist was just an ordinary human being, but he was called by God to prepare the way for people to receive the supernatural intervention of Jesus into their lives. In the fulfilment of God's plans and purpose for humanity there's always a part that He requires His people to pursue.

In our quest for divine healing today, there are things that only we can do. These include confession, repentance and forgiving of others. Then there are things that only God can do: these include the revelation of truth about our lives, His forgiving of our sinful beliefs and behaviours, His deliverance from spiritual oppression, His supernatural changing of human hearts, and His repair of the human spirit, soul and body. Some things are possible for us to do, and we need to press on and to do them, but some things are impossible for us, and so then it's over to God!

It's very likely that we have suffered negative experiences in our lives, but sometimes we need God's revelation to remind us of those times of wounding that remain unresolved, to recognise the past hurts that are still affecting us today. Often, and even more importantly, we need God to show us how we dealt with those painful times. If the effect and memory of these very real experiences were pushed away, this may turn out to be one of the significant root issues behind today's bouts of depression.

When there is a fault somewhere in the systems of our computer, it sometimes switches into what is termed a *safe mode*, still working but with a screen that is dumbed down from normal functioning. It seems that we can make similar unconscious choices to go into what we think will be a safe mode. We do this in order to protect ourselves from further hurt to the inner damaged place. Our part in the healing journey will then include a choice to face the 'pushed-away' places, knowing that Jesus is ready to help us in the process.

God's order for our lives does not include being disconnected from the painful experiences of life, but rather He desires that we resolve them with Him and accept the wounded places as hard but healed memories. To hide away or abandon a place within ourselves, in order to try and find our own means of comfort, is not His way. Those choices we made may be entirely understandable in the light of the pain that was suffered but, when viewed today from God's perspective, they were sinful choices and will require our repentance. It's very common for a wounded heart to also become a sinful heart through the inner decisions we make, perhaps unconsciously, to meet our own needs of protection and comfort.

A secular psychoanalyst, Sally Willis, with more than 30 years of experience in treating depression, wrote that she had come to the conclusion that it results from a way of unconsciously defending yourself against overwhelming thoughts and emotions, usually generated by childhood trauma. It's like a blanket over feelings that are unacceptable to the conscious mind.

Of course, this will not be the full explanation of the causes of this widespread disorder, but it strongly resonates with how many followers of Jesus have recognised the roots of their depression. They have found true healing through allowing

God into the deep inner wounds as well as into the ways in which they have sought to 'blanket' over the past. Coping with past pain, without God, invariably distorts the spiritual condition of our hearts.

Lucy's blanket

I was talking recently to *our friend Lucy* who has struggled over several decades with depression, triggered more recently by family tragedy but clearly rooted in childhood trauma. Interestingly, as far back as she could remember, she had been dependent on a small pink blanket to hide herself away and find a measure of comfort from the pain of parental dysfunction and disorder in the early years of her life.

Underneath that blanket this little girl had tried to shut out the noise of her drunken father and the cries of her younger brother who was looking to her for comfort. It was all too overwhelming. In fact, she remembered that under the blanket she had even sought death as a solution to her insoluble distress. As a little girl she had no real understanding of what she was asking for and, today, we can empathise with her desperate responses. However, the enemy gained an opportunity to get a grip on her life, through parental carelessness and Lucy's ways of trying to survive. For her, there seemed to be no way of dealing with such overwhelming issues except by fighting them off through trying to hide away.

It was a powerful breakthrough moment for Lucy when she was able to acknowledge and confess before the Lord the continued choice she had made to try and escape from life under the pink blanket. Sadly, it had actually been a covering of spiritual darkness over part of her life. She was then able to make a new choice to instead be hidden in Jesus, and this provided an amazing opportunity for light to be brought into the darkness. In effect, the little girl under the blanket was no longer left abandoned in frightening isolation and despair, but was now given safety in a new opportunity of divine comfort, especially in the previously overwhelmed places inside.

Facing the truth of hidden distress

This is also a good opportunity to share the story of *our friend Deirdre*. The first step in the process of God's healing in her life required her to face the reality of a very difficult past. She had never really felt a sense of joy or contentment in her life and could never understand why. To all outward appearances, in her early thirties, she had a good life, a good job, a good marriage and four beautiful children, but inside there was an emptiness and sadness that wouldn't go away.

Then in 2003, she unexpectedly met her aunt and uncle in an airport and the uncle made a move to lift her eighteen-month-old son out of the buggy she was pushing. Deirdre described how something snapped inside her. The problem was that this uncle had abused her when she was a little girl, and the incident in the airport took the lid off a contained past that she had tried hard to bury and forget. For the next nine years Dierdre's emotional health deteriorated to the point where antidepressant medication became necessary to stabilise her life.

There was increasing dosage of medication and an increasing sense of hopelessness, but then in 2012 she had the opportunity to go on a Christian healing retreat. She had reached rock-bottom in her life and her doctor was only able to suggest a different medication. On the retreat Deidre met with God at a completely new depth, and she was able to look at issues of forgiveness in a way that had been impossible before.

Up to that point in her life, Deidre had never understood what it meant to truly forgive someone or how it was possible to forgive something that you consider unforgiveable, in her case the sexual abuse of herself as a young child. Her only solution to the inner anger, bitterness, resentment, shame, and the overwhelming sense of worthlessness, was to bury all the feelings. That day on the retreat, as she forgave from her heart, God brought deep healing and deliverance, resulting in an extraordinary freedom from the depression she had been suffering. After consultation with her doctor there was no further need for the medication, and that has continued ever since. Jesus spoke some very remarkable words in John 8:31-32:

> *"If you continue in My word, then you are truly disciples of Mine; and you will know the truth, and the truth will make you free."*
>
> *NASB*

Deidre chose that day to believe in these words of Jesus and, as a result, she realised the truth of what had been at the root of her depression, and she acted on it. She also recognised the power of forgiveness and the truth of God's ability to heal. Here are her own words of how she feels today:

> "For too many years I believed the lie that if I forgave the person who had abused me then what was done didn't really matter. The truth is that it does matter but, when

we forgive, we are choosing to hand it over to God to allow Him to be the judge.

Over the years, there have been many layers to my healing and, while I can't say that it has been an easy journey (because in truth it has been very hard and challenging at times), I wouldn't trade one minute of the journey for the peace and joy God has now given me. I and many others are living proof that God is still in the business of restoring broken and shattered lives. The question for all of us is *are we prepared to make a choice to trust God and gain freedom from the wounds and hurts of the past?* I have truly seen that *I can do all things through Him who strengthens me (Philippians 4:13, NASB)*, and I give all glory to God."

Key points from this chapter

- From a secular perspective, the causes of depression are seen to be associated with personal temperament, the side effects of medical disorders and of prescribed medication, faulty nerve cell communications, genetic predisposition, and the consequence of life traumas.

- The medical response to depression, often essential to manage the deeply distressing symptoms, is mostly centred around talking therapies and antidepressants. Talking therapies seek to redirect the beliefs, thinking and behaviours of the patient, and to help them understand and accept their past. Antidepressant medication is intended to reorder the levels of neurotransmitters (such as serotonin) within the brain, as these chemicals have a significant effect on a person's mood.

- Recent medical research is also exploring an apparent link between inflammation in the body and the symptoms of depression. Inflammation occurs as a result an unconscious defensive reaction by the body, to situations deemed to be hostile to its well-being. Interestingly, this research also points to the fact that chronic inflammation in the body often results from unresolved past trauma.

- From a Christian perspective, the root causes of depression are likely to include the consequence of an ungodly spiritual inheritance, oppressive lifestyle choices, the effect of demonic intrusion and, in particular, damage to the human spirit from an unconscious disconnection with unresolved negative experiences of life in the past.

- God alone can see into the depths of our being. He alone fully understands the root causes and the triggers for the symptoms of depression. He alone will be able to touch and restore the deep places of damage in the human heart. However, we have an important part to play in the healing process. This starts by our seeking Him for the truth of the unresolved hurts of the past and an understanding of the way we responded to them. These buried hurts and our unconscious responses can be significant roots to the depression that we suffer today.

CHAPTER 3

God sees the precise place of inner despair

Nothing goes unnoticed by Jesus

We frequently see in the Psalms the writer challenging God for His apparent unconcern over the distress of His people.

> *Psalm 44:23-24... Arouse Yourself, why do You sleep, O Lord? Awake, do not reject us forever. Why do You hide Your face and forget our affliction and our oppression?*
>
> NASB

But, of course, an indifferent God is very far from the truth. He has always been concerned about every detail of our lives and we are made very aware of this in the records of how Jesus responded to the distress He witnessed in those around Him. As He walked on the earth, Jesus saw, and indeed He still sees, the despair that can fill the human heart. What is more, He came with the desire and the ability to restore the abundance of life that God intended for us all.

> *Matthew 9:35-36... Jesus was going through all the cities and villages, teaching in their synagogues and proclaiming the gospel of the kingdom, and healing every kind of disease and every kind of sickness. Seeing the people, He felt compassion for them, because they were distressed and dispirited like sheep without a shepherd.*
>
> *NASB*

He would have seen within many people the pain of spiritual isolation, which is strongly linked to depression. These feelings of abandonment are rooted deep in the human spirit, a part of our being we will seek to further understand in this chapter. Jesus knows the needs of every one of His followers, and what He spoke out to His first disciples He still speaks into our hearts today:

> *John 14:18... I will not leave you as orphans; I will come to you."*
>
> *NASB*

Depression is not just having a bad day

When major depression has gripped someone's life it doesn't help the person to hear others say, "Come on, snap out of it!" It's good to have supportive friends around, but even the writer of Proverbs recognised the futility of trying to "jolly" the sufferer of depression into a better mood.

> *Proverbs 25:20... Singing to a person who is depressed is like taking off his clothes on a cold day or like rubbing salt in a wound.*
>
> *GNB*

Thankfully, God looks deeper than the presenting symptoms and will not belittle the pain that is being felt. He knows where and why we are feeling the distress. Jesus has been to the depths of human despair and cried out to both His friends and His Father.

> *Matthew 26:38-39... Then He said to them, "My soul is deeply grieved to the point of death; remain here and keep watch with Me." And He went a little beyond them, and fell on His face and prayed, saying, "My Father, if it is possible, let this cup pass from Me; yet not as I will, but as You will."*
>
> *NASB*

Jesus demonstrates His intimate knowledge of human misery and His personal ability to overcome the extreme of despair, through the relationship with His Father. For that reason, we too can find true restoration from the grip of depression, when we utterly depend on Him.

The important difference between the trigger and the root cause

Current difficult life issues can, of course, strongly affect our mood, but if the 'down days' develop into a bout of major depression it is most likely that today's events are simply a trigger into much deeper causes. Stress and overwhelm from issues such as bereavement, divorce, job loss, moving house, financial distress or the menopause may be *the straw that breaks the camel's back*, unexpectedly touching into the hidden hurts of the past. Today's challenges can also surface the reality of how we have developed coping strategies to deal with the deeper unresolved negative experiences of life.

Sometimes, today's difficulty may not appear that significant, but it can perhaps be an unconscious reminder of an unresolved trauma from childhood. A good example of this was when *our friend Deirdre* unexpectedly met the uncle who had once abused her, and he had seemed to threaten her own eighteen-month-old child. This trigger was the start of Deidre's battle with depression, eventually overcome when the root issue of abuse was resolved with God. As already mentioned, it's not uncommon for the root causes of depression to be linked to times of isolation in early life. So, an experience today of unexpectedly finding oneself alone, for whatever reason, can trigger a connection to an abandoned, dark and unsafe part of ourselves within.

Pin-pointing the true hurting place

We saw in the first chapter that many of the symptoms of depression, such as low self-confidence and low self-worth, seem to point to very deep issues within the sufferer. It is clearly a disorder that profoundly disturbs a person's mental and physical well-being but is apparently rooted in damage from the past, which affects how they feel about themselves as a person. *Our friends*, who have shared testimony for this book, along with countless others who have suffered with depression, repeatedly mention the spiritual nature of this issue.

As I have read the stories of many people who describe what it's like to be in the depths of depression, I have been struck by their similarity. They describe a place within them in deep despair, and this is not simply the location of painful emotion but a place that carries distress and despair related to their very personhood. When we compare these verbal pictures from people today, with particular scriptures (for example the words of King David in his times of deep despair) we find that both descriptions are clearly looking at a disorder involving the soul and the spirit.

Let's look at some of these examples:

"It's like drowning."

> *Psalm 142:2-3a... I pour out my complaint before Him; I declare my trouble before Him. When my spirit was overwhelmed [or shrouded in darkness] within me, You knew my path.*
>
> *NASB*

"It's worse than the most intense physical discomfort."

> *Proverbs 18:14... The spirit of a man can endure his sickness, but as for a broken spirit who can bear it?*
>
> *NASB*

"It's like a heavy black cloak."

> *Psalm 143:3-4... The enemy pursues me, he crushes me to the ground; he makes me dwell in darkness like those long dead. So my spirit grows faint within me; my heart within me is dismayed.*
>
> *NIV*

"You try to correct the negative thoughts about yourself but end up building your prison."

> *Psalm 142:7a... Bring my soul out of prison, so that I may give thanks to Your name.*
>
> *NASB*

"It's like a sinkhole, a place to which all mental processes converge given the right circumstances."

> *Psalm 143:7... Answer me quickly, O Lord, my spirit fails; do not hide Your face from me, or I will become like those who go down to the pit.*
>
> *NASB*

"There is a feeling of terrible emptiness."

> *Job 17:1...My spirit is broken, my days are extinguished, the grave is ready for me.*
>
> *NASB*

"I want to cover myself up until it disappears."

> *Psalm 61:2,4b... From the end of the earth I call to You when my heart is faint... Let me take refuge in the shelter of your wings.*
>
> *NASB*

"I want to write myself out of the picture."

> *Psalm 42:5a... Why are you in despair, O my soul? And why have you become so disturbed within me?*
>
> *NASB*

Depression and spiritual darkness

The themes of heaviness and blackness are very common in the descriptions that people give for the deep feelings of despair associated with depression. Interestingly, the term "leaden paralysis" is still sometimes used by doctors to refer to the sensation of sufferers being weighed down, the heaviness of a body slow to respond. I can't help wondering if this was just what was being experienced by the man lowered down through the roof, a leaden paralysis, which Jesus recognised as being the result of deep and unresolved issues of guilt (Luke 5:17-20).

It's significant that *our friend Imogen*, when reflecting on the painful symptoms of her depression, said, "Worst of all, I felt surrounded by darkness." Winston Churchill and Samuel Johnson both called depression their "black dog". Whether they realised the significance of their words or not, they were clearly referring to a spiritual darkness rather than just an emotional darkness.

This spiritual darkness was also the experience of *our friend James*. He had grown up with aggressive rejection from his father and, as a result, he had a deep sense of worthlessness. Following a successful career in the Navy and despite becoming a Christian in 1976, James became more and more depressed.

> Triggered by concerns about his salvation, stressful situations at work and in his marriage, James found himself, in 1988, plunging into what he described later as "a black pit of hopelessness".

Even with heavy medication, James experienced terrifying panic attacks and he has described that time of his life as being "hell on earth". In the midst of this, the Lord gave him a Christian doctor, and several Christian brothers who stood with him in prayer through a time of overwhelming weakness and sadness. Then, at a Christian conference, James went forward for prayer and received from the Lord a spontaneous outburst of joyous laughter which remained with him for days.

This was an extraordinary breakthrough because he hadn't laughed for so many years. Of course, we will all have different experiences, but this was the particular way that God chose to start the process of healing for James.

Despite it being a slow journey, since that time James has walked with God into an increasing confidence in himself and his self-worth. There was much inner healing and deliverance along that path. James' image of God as Father, so damaged by the experience of his earthly father, was gradually transformed into the truth given in the Bible. James is a completely different person today as compared with that man who had been in the "black pit" of spiritual despair.

Let's for a moment reflect again on what God has proclaimed in the words of the prophet Isaiah, a promise for all His covenant people, words made a reality today through the sending of His Son, Jesus Christ.

> *Isaiah 61:3... [God has sent Me to] provide for those who grieve in Zion – to bestow on them a crown of beauty instead of ashes, the oil of joy instead of mourning, and a garment of praise instead of a* ***spirit of despair****. They will be called oaks of righteousness, a planting of the Lord for the display of his splendour.*
>
> *NIV*

The word *despair* in this verse is very interesting for our exploration of where the damage causing depression is truly rooted. Many descriptions of people's feelings associated with this disorder mention similar words to those used in the various Bible translations of this verse. A spirit of fainting, heaviness, discouragement, weakness and grief are clearly all descriptions of something dark and unbearable, deep inside our being. We need to look more fully into the reality of how the human spirit and human soul operate in the body.

The effect of a damaged human spirit on the whole body

Let's consider what Jesus says about the significance of damage in the human spirit. Here's a particularly important verse:

> *Luke 11:34-36... "Your eye is the lamp of your body. When your eyes are good, your whole body also is full of light. But when they are bad, your body also is full of darkness. See to it, then, that the light within you is not darkness. Therefore, if your whole body is full of light, and no part of it dark, it will be completely lighted, as when the light of a lamp shines on you."*
>
> *NIV.*

Those listening to Jesus would have been familiar with this other verse from the Old Testament:

> *Proverbs 20:27... The spirit of man is the lamp of the Lord, searching all the innermost parts of his being.*
>
> *NASB*

As we have seen, inner blackness or darkness are very common descriptions of the sense of profound despair associated with depression. In the verse above, from Luke chapter 11, Jesus is using a picture to describe the effect of dysfunction in the human spirit by comparing it with how the condition of the eye physically affects the whole body. Put simply, damaged eyes mean a lack of light entering the optical systems of the body; a damaged spirit means a lack of spiritual light entering the mind, will and emotions.

> The human spirit is intended by God to be a light and life source for the whole body, but this source is distorted when there is damage in the spirit from unresolved wounding or defilement from the past, often exacerbated by our coping choices in the present. The light source for the soul and body becomes darkened.

Even more distressing is the fact that, instead of bringing life into our being, the genuine emptiness and needs in the human spirit can seem to draw life out of us. Here's a very pertinent description by someone expressing the symptoms of depression: "It's a giant black cloud that will suck any kind of personality or positivity out of somebody. You are just left a shell."

Interestingly the Greek physician Hippocrates, considered an outstanding figure in the history of medicine, listed one of the most significant symptoms of depression as being how the sufferer looked "hollow-eyed". I suggest that his description was in fact pointing to the emptiness that comes from the human spirit, for many of those struggling with depression.

As we look through the Bible, we discover that there are many descriptions of how the human spirit can experience damage from the issues of life. It can be overwhelmed (Psalm 142:3), heavy or fainting (Isaiah 61:3), broken (Job 17:1), destitute (Matthew 5:3) and defiled (2 Corinthians 7:1). When a person is born again, the human spirit becomes alive to the Holy Spirit, experiencing *The Light of the world* (John 8:12) for the first time. However, when a sea bird is rescued from an oil-slick and is taken into an oil-free environment, it comes with the clinging oil and damage of the past. And so it is for each of us, when we are born again, the spiritual defilement and damage of the past still needs God's cleansing and restoration.

> *2 Corinthians 7:1… Therefore, having these promises, beloved, let us cleanse ourselves from all defilement of flesh and spirit, perfecting holiness in the fear of God.*
>
> *NASB*

Understanding the soul and spirit

I came across these words in one of the many secular articles that I have read on the topic of depression, a description that points to dysfunctional inner workings of the mind. The writer didn't know the reality of the human soul and spirit but was clearly recognising some kind of dark and disordered inner turmoil:

> "The mysterious nature of depression has led some to argue that it has a basis in the functioning of the mind, a functioning that is disrupted and made malignant."

We need to look at God's design for the function and interaction of our soul and spirit, and we need to consider how a disruption to that Godly order could be at the root of the symptoms of depression. The Bible clearly explains that each one of us has not only a human soul but also a human spirit. Here is one of many scriptures that refer to these two precious aspects of our being:

> *Hebrews 4:12... For the word of God is living and active and sharper than any two-edged sword, and piercing as far as the division of soul and spirit, of both joints and marrow, and able to judge the thoughts and intentions of the heart.*
>
> *NASB*

The picture given to us here is that the soul can be compared to the joints in the body, whereas the spirit is like the marrow inside the bones. The marrow, where blood cells are produced, is a hidden place within us that gives physical life to the whole body. The human spirit has a similar function: it is the part of us which God has given to impart spiritual life. Indeed, the Bible tells us that when the human spirit leaves the body there is death (Ecclesiastes 12:7, James 2:26). What is perhaps more significant for our understanding of depression is that the human spirit holds the key to our awareness of personal identity.

> *1 Corinthians 2:11a... It is only a person's own spirit within him that knows all about him.*
>
> *GNB*

In contrast, the joints in the body (mentioned in the verse from Hebrews) are the main way in which everyone physically expresses the life that is within them, for example by speech and movement. So, we are being told that the human soul is the place within us where we express the reality of our lives in thinking, decision-making and feelings. Even Jesus, in His humanity, spoke out these activities of His soul.

> *John 12:27-28a... "Now My soul has become troubled; and what shall I say, 'Father, save Me from this hour'? But for this purpose I came to this hour. 'Father, glorify Your name'."*
>
> NASB

So how do these two aspects of our being relate to each other? Depression clearly affects our soul (the mind, will and emotions) but many of the symptoms we have highlighted point also to a deeper damage in the human spirit, the place within us intended to carry the confidence of our unique God-given identity.

Unhealthy interaction between the soul and spirit

Even in the secular world, it is being recognised more and more that depression is the result, not just of the things that have damaged us (for example trauma or childhood deprivation) but, perhaps more importantly, of the unconscious way in which we have responded to that damage.

God intended that every one of us should be strong in spirit, nurtured by Godly parents and knowing a secure upbringing, right from conception. It's significant that the Bible records for us the particular need for this growth in John the Baptist in his early years.

> *Luke 1:80a... And the child continued to grow and to become strong in spirit.*
>
> NASB

For followers of Jesus today, God has provided the opportunity for us to have a deep confidence in our spirit, affirmed by the Holy Spirit, that we are children of God. This truth can then direct all the thoughts, feelings and decisions of our soul, allowing us to walk securely into our God-given destiny.

> *Romans 8:16... The Spirit Himself testifies with our spirit that we are children of God...*
>
> *NASB*

Sadly, for many of us, there have been traumas in life and distortions to God's intended plan for our developmental years. This damage, received in our human spirit, means that we may not be receiving such a confident message in the soul, but rather a troubling sense of insecurity, anger, inadequacy, overwhelm, abandonment, helplessness and discomfort. We have previously noted that brokenness at the core of our being is indeed unbearable, so clearly described in Proverbs.

> *Proverbs 18:14...The spirit of a man can endure his sickness, but as for a broken spirit who can bear it?*
>
> *NASB*

Without a clear knowledge of the Lord's ability to help us and restore us, how are we to cope with these deep and unbearable feelings? Here, I suggest, is a pivotal moment of decision for the interaction between the soul and spirit, if we make a subconscious choice to hide the unbearable place under a 'blanket', as described by *our friend Lucy*. However understandable, this was her soulish attempt to resolve the deep distress of the heart, to shut away the perceived weakness, to hide a vulnerable identity, to be strong, to survive, in fact to depend on human effort and human wisdom.

> *James 3:15... Such wisdom does not come down from heaven; it belongs to the world, it is unspiritual [soulish] and demonic.*
> *GNB*

"But at the time I didn't know any other way to survive"

Without awareness of God's ability to rescue us, perhaps as young children in an unbelieving household, self-protection was completely understandable. As we become followers of Jesus later in life, this suppression of inner weakness, anger or shame, for example, can even seem biblically justified. We are called to walk in a way no longer ruled by sin, indeed we should be dead to the pull of sin (Romans 6:11). However, the Bible does not call us to consider any part of our created being as dead either to ourselves or to God, as a way of suppressing the pain of the past. God comes to us today, without condemnation of our past coping mechanisms and defending behaviours, to give us the opportunity to resolve the hurt of the past with Him, rather than in our own strength.

The result of our using ungodly soulish self-control is that, instead of our soul being given life and direction from our human spirit, the soul is in fact crushing the life out of our spirit, locking this part of ourselves into despair and spiritual darkness. When the despair of this dark place breaks through to the surface, triggered by some challenging event of today, the painful symptoms of depression can suddenly overwhelm us. This is what the world refers to as a mood disorder, but its origin very likely lies in a damaged spirit. Thankfully, in this very painful place, we can begin to do just as David did, we can cry out to the Lord to restore us from the unbearable inner disorder.

> *Psalm 143:7-8... Answer me quickly, O Lord, my spirit fails; do not hide Your face from me, or I will be like those who go down to the pit. Let me hear Your lovingkindness in the morning; for I trust in You; teach me the way in which I should walk; for to You I lift up my soul.*
>
> *NASB*

Jesus provides the only true safety for resolving spiritual damage

Most secular medical practitioners certainly recognise the depth of the underlying causes of depressive disorder, but they cannot offer a spiritual perspective or a spiritual solution. We are truly grateful for all their pursuit of effective treatment, but there is no department in the hospital for binding up a broken heart or setting a captive free from spiritual bondage. Indeed, there can be problems if someone connects with an abandoned place of despair inside but is not provided with a safe emotional and spiritual solution. Here is a comment from someone who had undergone secular psychoanalysis, which had been seeking to connect them with the place of underlying distress:

"I was able to feel pure sadness for the first time in many years. I had been fighting it, denying it, resisting it. Depression is sadness you have been fighting. It is sadness plus anxiety. To experience pure sadness is a relief."

It was good for this person to finally recognise and to face the emotion that had been so long denied, while he was trying to resolve the inner pain his own way. However, this is exactly the moment when the touch of Jesus is so desperately needed to deal with everything that has been out of line with God on the inside.

> *Isaiah 53:6... All of us like sheep have gone astray, each of us has turned to his own way; but the Lord has caused the iniquity of us all to fall on Him.*
>
> *NASB*

Depression is not just caused by sadness we have been fighting but by all the painful emotions which remain as a hidden part of us inside. As followers of Jesus, we truly have a safe way of connecting with inner emotions and darkness, allowing Him to bring comfort and freedom to places that the enemy would, no doubt, like to retain under his control. Interestingly, the Word of God encourages us to deny the devil any opportunity of keeping the feelings of past injustice buried in spiritual darkness.

> *Ephesians 4:26-27...Be angry, and yet do not sin; do not let the sun go down on your anger, and do not give the devil an opportunity.*
>
> *NASB*

Key points from this chapter

- The medical profession cannot look into the heart of man and see the root causes of depression, but Jesus can, if we ask Him.

- Although frequently there are circumstances that trigger a bout of depression, these are rarely the actual cause of the disorder. The trigger can be the "last straw", the stressful issue of today that is sufficient to plummet us into the normally hidden place of darkness in our lives.

- Remarkably, the many translations of Isaiah 61:3, when put together, reflect very accurately the way people describe many of the paralysing feelings of depression: a sense of despair, heaviness, weakness, darkness or blackness. This verse clearly points to the spiritual nature of the issue.

- The Bible describes the heart of man as being the place of interaction between the human soul and the human spirit (Hebrews 4:12). When this interaction is not in line with God's created order, through soulish control, there can be significant damage to the human spirit. This can take the form of brokenness, overwhelm and spiritual defilement.

- Unhealed damage in the human spirit inevitably affects the physical body, sometimes in a way that can be unbearable (Proverbs 18:14). However, in Jesus, there is a safe way of reaching and restoring that damaged place, and of bringing God's order back into the whole body.

CHAPTER 4

God sees every moment of our past and present

Where in our life-story is the depression rooted?

Jeremiah 1:5a... "Before I formed you in the womb I knew you." NASB

We all have a past, and our lives today are affected by every second of that past, however much we may wish to bury it. God reminds Jeremiah that His knowledge of this prophet's life started even before conception. If we trust that the Lord wants the very best for us, it's surely a comfort to know that not one moment of our lives has gone unnoticed by Him. What is even more comforting is the fact that, while He will not change our life-history, He does have the willingness and the ability to repair the spiritual damage of every incident that has deeply afflicted our hearts.

Not everyone thinks that looking into the past is a good idea. I recently read this statement from a secular therapist dealing with the issue of depression in people's lives, "Digging up emotional pains from the past just increases your misery. You just reinforce the negative experiences at the expense of the positive ones."

If we had no way of truly resolving those past hurts, then this advice might well be of value. However, for those walking with Jesus, the situation is completely different. Firstly, we do not have to dig up the past but rather we can ask Him to reveal those times that have been left without His comfort and resolution. Secondly, the therapist who made the statement above was unaware of the divine power of forgiveness to radically heal the inner wounds in our lives. In forgiving others who have hurt us, and in receiving God's complete forgiveness for the serious mistakes that we have made, there can be true closure on the negative issues of the past. They do not have to be repeatedly revisited. As an example of the need to find true closure to past hurts, for some of those repeatedly suffering from seasonal affective disorder (SAD), I wonder if they are being unconsciously reminded of a dark incident in their lives that was connected with a particular time of year. Thankfully, God is outside of time and can see the fulness of our life-story, all the good times and the bad times, and He can help us bring closure.

In this chapter we will be looking at damaging events of the past, as well as the unhelpful life-choices that we have made in trying to resolve those past issues. It's important to recognise that both of these can be significant roots to today's episodes of depression. We are seeing that depression is, in fact, not so much the consequence of the things that have happened to us in our lives but probably much more the consequence of how we have dealt with those things.

The reality of our inner needs and how these have, or have not, been met

The needs of the human heart are recognised by those involved with psychiatric care, at least to some extent. Therapists do understand that, where those needs have not been met, it leaves significant voids in our sense of personhood. These unmet needs would include a lack of security, a lack of parental affirmation, a lack of self-worth or a lack of purpose, for example. They realise that such voids can have clear links with strong negative thinking and the symptoms of depression.

As previously mentioned, many secular therapists believe that any deficit of these deep needs of the human heart can be resolved through our own inherent ability, provided we learn the necessary techniques which tend to vary according to the particular school of therapy. But depending just on our human capability to resolve the unmet needs of the heart, without seeking God's ways, is a recipe for ultimate failure. We were designed to know Him as the only true answer to the cry of the heart for provision and protection.

We also need to remember that there is an enemy, the devil, who rules over a domain of fallen angels and unclean spirits. These are all bent on doing damage to human life, wherever there is license due to our opposition to the ways of God.

> *1 Peter 5:6-9... Humble yourselves, then, under God's mighty hand, so that He will lift you up in His own good time. Leave all your worries with Him, because He cares for you. Be alert, be on the watch! Your enemy, the Devil, roams around like a roaring lion, looking for someone to devour. Be firm in your faith and resist him, because you know that your*

> *fellow believers in all the world are going through the same kind of sufferings.*
>
> GNB

Wounds, sins and demons have all had opportunity to damage human lives, and we shall see that letting God reveal hidden and unresolved past wounding really does move us along the road out of major depression. We have already recorded that many people have unconsciously put some form of blanket over the place of wounding, only to find that it has become a very dark and despairing part of their being. It may remain hidden much of the time but can intrude into their lives at times of vulnerability causing bouts of depression that, for a while, can overwhelm them. Any part of our lives left in darkness becomes an opportunity for spiritual oppression. However, Jesus can see into the dark and He is ready to shine His light wherever we give Him permission.

Countless lives have been affected by very painful wounding

It's interesting to look at the early life of someone like Winston Churchill, who was a British prime minister during the second world war. He was eventually very open about his bouts of depression, which he referred to as his "black dog". Despite being part of a privileged family, he had had a very dysfunctional childhood, which had surely been very crushing to his spirit. There was a very cold relationship with his parents, particularly with his father from whom he received minimal affirmation, and he was raised mostly by a nanny. At the age of seven, Winston was sent from the relative stability of the home nursery to a boarding school where he experienced extreme loneliness and a brutal regime of discipline and flogging. He later commented with a somewhat bitter tone, "I was no more consulted about leaving home than I had been about coming into the world." He described his father, who died when Winston was aged twenty, as being deeply disappointed with him.

From accounts of the later life of Winston Churchill, we can see that he was a man of very strong character and determination, but it seems that the legacy of a crushed spirit from childhood was never fully resolved. This significantly contributed to the depression that was always there in the background of his life, ready to be triggered by particular life-circumstances.

The Bible is full of stories of people bringing their life-struggles before God. The amazing story of Job records a man suffering huge trauma and subsequently moving into more and more despair, while, at the same time, crying out to God for an understanding of why he was experiencing such apparent injustice.

> *"My spirit is broken, my days are extinguished, the grave is ready for me." Job 17:1,*
>
> *NASB*

Not until Job surrenders to the fact that God knows best, does he finally receive divine restoration. The journey of Job might well be considered an extreme example of a traumatic life-journey, but it highlights for us the significance of finding true peace and reconciliation with God. In all the uncertainties of our lives, such peace really can result in the inner restoration that we all long for. In the end it was recognising the rightness of God's wisdom, rather than his own, that was the breakthrough for Job.

> *"Therefore I have declared that which I did not understand... I will ask You, and You instruct me... Therefore I retract, and repent in dust and ashes." Job 42: 3,4,6,*
>
> *NASB*

It's interesting to note that Sigmund Freud, the founder of secular psychoanalysis, linked depression with unresolved childhood loss or parental rejection, when he observed that the symptoms were frequently very similar to those of bereavement. He believed that we are somehow compelled to repeat the deep despair of the past where it has not yet been resolved.

How precious it is that God understands all these things in minute detail, and He has so clearly stated in His word that He has the solution... *The oil of gladness instead of mourning (Isaiah 61:3, NASB).*

Some of us who witnessed television pictures shortly after the fall of communism in Romania in 1989 will never forget the lifeless appearance of the children who had been abandoned in government orphanages throughout the country. The plight of these children was well publicised and seemed unexpectedly shocking at the time but, sadly, it has become clear recently that childhood abuse of every kind is far more widespread than was recognised just a few decades ago.

A study of more than two thousand 18-year-olds, published

in *The Lancet Psychiatry* in February 2019, found that nearly a third had experienced significant trauma in childhood (such as assault, sexual assault, injury and family trauma). A quarter of these young adults had then developed symptoms of post-traumatic stress disorder (PTSD). More than half of those who developed PTSD had also experienced a major depressive episode, and one in five had attempted suicide.

There is little doubt that people exposed to trauma-induced stress in the early years of life are more likely to develop mood disorders as adults. When someone feels threatened, the body activates a biological response designed to protect the individual from events that may endanger survival. As we have already seen, there are strong links between this response to trauma and a vulnerability to disorders such as depression, when such trauma is left unresolved. The body systems are still sustaining a chronic defensive response.

People will continue to struggle with the biological effects of unhealed emotional and spiritual brokenness unless they have found the One who can reach into the places of darkness and distress. It's important that we keep highlighting this key verse:

> *Isaiah 61:1... The Spirit of the Sovereign Lord is upon me, because the Lord has anointed me to preach good news to the poor. He sent me to bind up the broken-hearted, to proclaim freedom for the captives and release from darkness for prisoners.*
> *NIV*

The importance of spiritual inheritance

Depression does appear to run in families. This can of course be a consequence of learned behaviour from watching how our parents coped with the difficult issues of their lives, but it seems to be more connected with an inherited trait. There is an interesting field of study called epigenetics. This recognises that, while the genes we inherit are not themselves necessarily changed by the behaviour of our ancestors, the way those genes function may well be pre-programmed by their choices. In some people, the inherited way genes switch on and off, giving instructions to the cells of the body, may be the cause of a malfunction of the transmission of serotonin, one of the chemicals affecting our mood.

I'm tempted to say here that it's inevitable that science will gradually catch up to be consistent with the many truths stated in the Word of God!

> *Exodus 20:5… "I, the Lord your God, am a jealous God, visiting the iniquity of the fathers on the children, on the third and the fourth generations of those who hate Me."*
>
> *NASB*

This verse describes the distortion to our whole being caused by the defiled spiritual inheritance we receive from the very moment of conception. The Bible is very clear about the damaging spiritual significance of the way of life of our ancestors and our need to be set free from the effects that this can have on our lives.

> *1 Peter 1:18a… For you know what was paid to set you free from the worthless manner of life handed down by your ancestors.*
>
> *GNB*

Hannah's unhelpful inheritance

Inherited disorder was certainly the experience of *our friend Hannah*. She had suffered from low-level depression all her life, with occasional bouts of major depression, triggered by specific family traumas. She began to walk with Jesus into an understanding of the roots of her problem and realised that depression had been a major issue with many of her past family members.

It became clear that a pivotal moment for the family had been a major depression suffered by her great grandfather. Through the disease of tuberculosis, he had lost two sons and a daughter over a period of just two months. After a few years of trying to deal with the loss, he had had a breakdown, was admitted to a psychiatric hospital and died at the age of 59. He had been a coastguard, helping to save lives of those at sea, and he had apparently found it intolerable that he was unable to save the lives of his sick children. Hannah remembered that while she was growing up, she was told that her great grandfather had died of a broken heart.

His time in psychiatric care was kept a secret and never talked about in the family. This was mostly because of the shame attached to his needing to be in, what was then called, a mental hospital. The effect of this hidden family loss and shame surfaced in Hannah's grandmother, during periods of serious depression when she also needed psychiatric care. The same happened with Hannah's great aunt, and then more specifically with her mother who, soon after Hannah's birth, suffered prolonged post-natal depression. Unusually, Hannah has strong memories of the early disappointment, evident in her mother, over Hannah being a girl and not a boy. She also has clear memories of her mother's complete lack of nurturing ability and she can recall the gloomy location of her large wooden cot in the corner of a downstairs room.

Reflecting on these memories, Hannah described it all recently as having been "born into darkness and depression". As I write that comment from Hannah, I'm reminded of the words of King David:

> *Psalm 51:5-6… Behold, I was brought forth in iniquity, and in sin my mother conceived me. Behold, You desire truth in the innermost being, and in the hidden part You will make me know wisdom.*
>
> *NASB*

Iniquity is a word that here describes the inherited spiritual condition into which David was born, the family heritage that was out of line with God's order. This exactly describes Hannah's situation, a family history that God revealed to her as she sought to understand her personal struggles with depression. There had certainly been many traumas in her own life causing deep distress, but these triggers clearly overlaid a much deeper family disorder of inherited and unresolved grief and shame.

As Hannah recognised the effect of her mother's depression on her own early life, she was able to forgive the whole family for allowing these unspoken and unresolved issues to be continued down the family line. God has done an amazing work of healing in Hannah, and she has learned to recognise the authority she has in Jesus to combat the momentary feelings of despair and disappointment when they occasionally still arise. Here are some recent words from Hannah:

> "God wants us to have victory over the areas that keep us from fulfilling His plan and purposes for our lives – depression can be such a monster to trap us from going anywhere, until we recognise and deal with its cause."

The importance of parental covering

It's very likely that the depression experienced by Winston Churchill, and indeed by countless other sufferers, can be traced back to inadequate spiritual covering in childhood. God designed us to need the certainty of protection as we grew up, particularly in the deep place of our human spirit, the core location of our personal identity.

Many children experience the distress of absent parents, abusive parents, careless parents, aggressive parents or controlling parents. Such issues in the family home not only cause emotional damage but leave the human spirit of a child feeling extremely unsafe, however much he or she finds ways of coping with the distress. Already very emotionally distant from his parents, Winston's unhappy experience at boarding school at the age of seven, will have been key to his inner feelings of abandonment and to his dissociative coping behaviours that gave opportunity to the "black dog" of his later depression.

Our friend Iris had a very difficult and unsafe childhood, in a family where her father had a serious alcohol problem. This resulted in the constant loss of his job and the family being moved on. Incredibly, by the age of nine Iris had attended over 50 different schools! There was little opportunity for her to make any lasting friends and indeed the whole family was shunned by neighbours due to her father's violent outbursts.

The situation became even worse when her mother left home and, from the age of fourteen, Iris began to experience sexual abuse from both her father and her uncle. Interestingly, she later found out that there had clearly been previous abuse in the family line. This horrendous situation at home continued for her up to the age of sixteen when the family were evicted due to rent arrears, and Iris was finally able to leave. She then lived with her granny and began a more contented life, eventually getting married, moving to Ireland and, in 1980, becoming a Christian. Very shortly after, symptoms of serious depression began, and she was prescribed the antidepressant medication, Prozac. She was soon taking sleeping tablets and finding that the antidepressants were having less and less effect.

Iris describes this period of her life as a time of just existing, not living. She wasn't sleeping, she lived in fear of the dark and fear of men. She felt as if her past had come back to haunt her. Then unexpectedly in 1989, with encouragement from a friend, she went on a Christian healing retreat at Ellel Grange. It was here that she began the long journey of forgiving her father for the abuse, and also her mother for leaving her so unprotected. For the first time in her life Iris began to feel a sense of freedom, and she has walked into more and more healing over the years since that time.

She no longer needs any medication for depression, treatment that had provided some welcome relief at times but had in fact masked the real issues. Iris can say today that, without any doubt, Jesus has restored her to life and peace. She knows that the Lord is her true Protector, and that now the inner fighting for self-protection has ceased. The spiritual covering that should have been provided by her parents has now been provided by God Himself, through His miraculous intervention.

[Recommended book: *God's Covering* by David Cross, ISBN 9781852404857]

Easy footholds for the enemy – false religion and the occult

In exploring the roots of depression, I have already mentioned that we cannot ignore the reality of demonic oppression. Despite this, we need to be very careful not to assume that the powers of darkness are necessarily responsible for all the symptoms of this distressing disorder. However, we know that the enemy is always on the prowl, looking for opportunity to steal something of our God-given destiny.

Together with other aspects of poor covering in a family, any parental involvement in the occult or false religion will inevitably leave children very exposed to spiritual damage. We shall see in a later chapter the effect that spiritualism in the home had on the life of *our friend Anthony*. Family or personal involvement in the occult or false religion gives the powers of darkness license to bring at least spiritual oppression to those affected if not a significant opening to major depression.

From a biblical perspective, all religious practice that is not centred on surrender to Jesus will have a negative spiritual effect on the participant. We can respect the sincerity of those involved in other world religions, but we cannot agree to the virtue of these practices to bring them wellbeing. For followers of Jesus, they must be described as false religions, giving opportunity for spiritual darkness that is the domain of unclean spirits.

There is no born-again experience for the human spirit on any pathway except in Jesus Christ. Without Him, the human heart remains in a condition of isolation and fear, even if unrealised by the person affected. Many religious practices can seem attractive in providing a way of coping with inner wounding, but such activity can never meet the true needs of the heart, and a "black dog" is always waiting for the opportunity to move in.

> *1 Corinthians 10:20... The sacrifices of pagans are offered to demons, not to God, and I do not want you to be participants with demons.*
>
> *NIV*

For a Christian, the occult can be defined as the pursuit of supernatural power outside of the authority of Jesus. Such pursuit inevitably attracts the powers of darkness which, without our having the ability to discern, may appear to provide an antidote to unmet needs in our lives. However, they will always be spiritually disabling, as opposed to the enabling power that comes from the Holy Spirit when we follow the commands of Jesus. In Acts, chapter 8, we see that Simon the magician came face to face with this challenge when he experienced the power of the Holy Spirit operating through Peter. Sadly, he was unwilling to seek God's true cleansing from his past occult involvement and Peter recognised the unresolved demonic hold on Simon's life.

> *Acts 8:23... "For I see that you are full of bitterness and captive to sin."*
>
> *NIV*

It's extraordinary how often a practice such as yoga is recommended by doctors and therapists as a solution to problems such as anxiety and depression. The roots of yoga, however much these are dismissed by modern practitioners, are clearly founded in the occult and false religion. The techniques are intended to make the participant more receptive to a realm of spiritual influence. Sadly, that influence can only come from the enemy and, for some, it will bring oppression and possibly demonic occupation. The evil one is very able to present the appearance of peace for a season, while concealing his underlying grip on the life of someone engaged in occult practice.

Acknowledging past involvement in false religion or the occult will be an important step for some of those seeking release from the grip of depression. God is always ready to extend His forgiveness and to cleanse us from any oppressive defilement from the enemy which is affecting our lives today.

Unhelpful lifestyle choices in response to the traumas of life

When bad things have affected us, particularly in our early lives, we naturally adopt coping strategies to minimise the pain and to seek protection from further hurt. Ideally, we would have reached out to God for His comfort, but if we didn't know Him at the time of our need, our sinful nature will have pressed us into beliefs and behaviours that were not God's ways for us. These can be lifestyles that give the enemy opportunity to spiritually empower the bad choices we have made.

Childhood comfort behaviours can develop later into compulsive practices, for example alcohol, comfort eating, excessive working, internet addiction, drugs or sexual promiscuity. Sadly, every one of these will just worsen the inner pain and be, in themselves, another contributor to bouts of depression. Alcohol is certainly a common and very tempting response to bouts of depression, but after a short period of mild euphoria, alcohol simply acts as a depressant just adding to the problem.

In February 2019, researchers from McGill University and the University of Oxford published results of an analysis of use of cannabis among adolescents over the previous 25 years. They found that use of the drug was associated with a significant increased risk of depression and suicide in adulthood. The statistics showed there to be around 60,000 such cases in the UK and about 400,000 in the US. Medically, it is believed that the likely cause of this link is the active ingredient in cannabis, THC, which is thought to have a lasting effect on the neurodevelopment of adolescent brains.

It's also important to record that high strength cannabis is known to give similar symptoms to certain hallucinatory drugs which cause out-of-body experiences or "trips". Whatever chemical disorder is taking place in the body, it's apparent from a spiritual perspective, that drugs of a psychedelic nature can cause a breaking in the God-intended integrity of the soul and spirit, leaving an opportunity for spiritual defilement and oppression.

Loving the sinner whom God has created but hating the sin that has robbed their lives

We need to be very careful when seeking to help someone struggling with depression not to add unnecessary guilt to their distress, by highlighting the wrong choices that they have made in their lives. However, at the right time, it will be important, for some people, to face the reality of any self-induced damage. For example, the chemical trauma of recreational drugs and the resulting spiritual and emotional consequence that this has had on their lives cannot be ignored.

With a heart full of love and compassion, Jesus did not shy away from confronting people with how their personal sin could affect their wellbeing. To a man who had been disabled for thirty-eight years, and who had received remarkable healing from Jesus, there were still some stern words from the Healer:

> *John 5:14... Afterwards Jesus found him in the temple and said to him, "Behold, you have become well; do not sin anymore, so that nothing worse happens to you."*
>
> *NASB.*

Countless precious lives have been severely damaged by life-choices seeking to alleviate inner pain. I was recently reading the testimony of an American lady called Laura Perry. She has a remarkable story of a desperate journey of struggling with her biological gender due to childhood trauma. She made a series of choices to "transition" to be a male, through hormone treatment, a double mastectomy and having all her reproductive organs removed.

Sadly, nothing brought her the inner peace that she craved, and sexual promiscuity became an increasing addiction. Attending LGBT meetings just seemed to add to the distress, and she made this comment in her testimony:

> "We thought these people [at the meetings] were the most depressed people in the world. We could not see the connection, that it was because transgenderism will lead to depression, because it's not real. It is a lie from the pit of hell. You cannot change your gender. It's just not biologically possible."

Laura, who had made the choice to call herself Jake, eventually found Jesus and began to walk in the truth of her God-given identity, allowing her life to be completely transformed. She gradually dealt with the issues of childhood trauma, chose to fully embrace her feminine gender after much heart-searching, and she is at last at peace.

I have mentioned this testimony because we are living in days of aggressive promotion of an ideology of sexual rights. Activist groups are seeking to normalise and legitimise sexual lifestyle choices that are not the truth of how God intended our lives to be. Any life-choice, which results in living a lie, as compared with the plumb line of God's order, will lead to spiritual oppression and the likelihood of mood disorders such as major depression.

The world says that we should accept every lifestyle on the grounds of equality, freedom and inclusivity. However, the Word of God says that many of these choices are simply a form of rebellion and are life-destroying, albeit rooted in very understandable attempts to deal with unresolved inner pain.

> *Proverbs 14:12… There is a way that seems right to a man, but its end is the way of death.*
>
> *NASB*

Getting rid of the weight of guilt

> *Psalm 32:3-4… When I kept silent about my sin, my body wasted away through my groaning all day long. For day and night Your hand was heavy upon me; my vitality was drained away as with the fever heat of summer.*
>
> *NASB*

The Word of God is not there to condemn us, and certainly not when we are struggling with depression. However, King David describes here the experience of guilt, a God-ordained way of helping us to recognise the reality of sin. The distress he expresses is very similar to that experienced by sufferers of depression, and indeed a persistent feeling of guilt is one of the symptoms that doctors recognise in diagnosing the disorder.

Of course, the issue may well be false guilt because of an irrational sense of responsibility for some shameful incident or supposedly unforgiveable sin. Then it's important that we make sure to bring these concerns to the Lord for His truth and restoration. However, we do need to recognise that sometimes our wrongdoings of the past have been buried rather than fully resolved with God. Such disconnection from the reality of sin, often lost in a subconscious choice, will inevitably weigh heavily on us, as David discovered. God's complete forgiveness is available for everyone, but that forgiveness brings no freedom unless it has been fully appropriated through our confession, our repentance, and our receiving of His mercy.

Key points from this chapter

- Every moment of our life-history has been seen by God and He is able, today, to bring healing to the hurting places of the past.

- He has given mankind freewill choice which means that, sadly, human sinfulness has caused much wounding in the heart of man. For many people, the deep needs of the heart have not been met as God intended. This has left marks of spiritual damage, places of distress and darkness that can sometimes overwhelm us today, leading to symptoms of depression.

- God has seen the times of trauma in our lives, poor parental covering and abusive relationships. He has seen how we have sought to cope with these painful times in our own strength, perhaps resorting to behaviours that have become compulsive, such as comfort eating, alcohol, drugs or sexual promiscuity. He will never condemn us, but he does come to us with His offer of forgiveness, resolution for the hurt of the past, and freedom from the grip of the enemy.

- For some people there has been a defiled spiritual inheritance down the family line that has predisposed them to bouts of depression, particularly when life has been challenging. Thankfully, this inheritance can be cleansed by the Lord, and His restoration of our lives secured.

- All occult practice and false religions open a wide door to oppression from the powers of darkness, whether that has been the practices of our family or our personal involvement. For some, this can be a driver of depression. God is ready to set us free from every work of spiritual darkness when we come to Him in personal repentance and when we forgive those who have left us spiritually vulnerable.

CHAPTER 5

Crossroads on God's road map to recovery

The destination of freedom and how to get there

Most of us have become familiar with the satnav, the device we use in our cars to help navigate our journeys. It knows where we are, but we need to start the navigation process by entering the required destination. The healing ministry of Jesus can be described as the restoration of God's order both in our bodies and in the life that we lead. For those walking with Him, this is also our destination if we are suffering with depression: the return of God's created order and therefore His peace.

We are usually happy to go along with the method by which the satnav guides us in our car, advising us only of the next junction and how to negotiate that step of the journey. In the restoration journey that God has planned for His children, we may be less comfortable with only knowing the next turning He is asking us to take. We may wish that we had the whole picture of how to get to the desired place of peace, but God seems to prefer to work on a "need-to-know" basis. He simply asks us to respond to His next directive and to trust Him with the rest. Each intersection is a time of deeper revelation and an opportunity to respond to His instruction, if we choose to do so.

David, the shepherd and the king, had remarkable confidence in walking step by step with the Lord. David would seek His direction, especially when struggling through particular times of darkness and spiritual oppression.

> *Psalm 139:11-12... If I say, "Surely the darkness will overwhelm me, and the light around me will be night," even the darkness is not dark to You, and the night is as bright as the day. Darkness and light are alike to You.*
>
> *NASB.*

If we take a wrong turning, there is no condemnation from God, although it might result in a slightly longer journey and a need for some "recalculation", just as we hear from the voice on the satnav!

God's part and our part in the healing journey

Let's look at the likely decision points, the crossroads along the journey out of depression. These are given as pointers for those struggling with this issue, but also as a guide to those carers seeking to walk alongside them. It's very likely that this challenging journey with the Lord may well, at least for some time, be with the assistance of prescribed medication, to help in stabilising the traveller. With this in mind, we can ask the Lord to deal with any effects of the medication that would interfere with His roadmap for restoration.

Apart from the starting and the finishing place, there is no fixed order for the suggested steps on this journey with the Lord. If we allow Him to direct us, He will lead us to whatever is the next important intersection where His truth can be revealed, and our choices can be made. He will encourage us to do those things that are possible for us, to be open, to be forgiving and to be repentant. As we do our part, He will do the things that are impossible for us, such as bringing His revelation and His healing.

The starting place: sharing the problem

> *Psalm 42:5... Why are you in despair, O my soul? And why have you become disturbed within me? Hope in God, for I shall again praise Him for the help of His presence.*
>
> *NASB*

It can be very hard to admit to ourselves, and even more so to our loved ones, that we are experiencing sustained feelings of utter hopelessness and despair. Whether we realise it or not, all of our close family will have been affected by the moods of depression that have troubled us. Therefore, it's important that, in some measure, all of them are able to be involved in the resolution.

When the problem is shared, the very best thing that the family and carers can do, at least to start with, is to just be a listening ear, offering sympathy but not quick solutions or religious platitudes. Simply validating the sufferer's experiences can be a huge step in starting the journey of healing. As a friend or family member, don't offer advice if you are not being asked. Perhaps the best response is, "How can I help, or how can I make it easier for you?" Here are a few more general suggestions for carers walking this journey:

- Help the sufferer to understand this is a real illness not a personal weakness.
- Encourage patience.
- Encourage and praise good routines in eating, sleeping and exercise.
- Encourage relationship with the wider family and with friends.
- Encourage and praise healthy social and creative activities.
- Don't be afraid to discuss suicidal feelings.
- Offer to visit a doctor with them.
- Encourage professional help, where management of symptoms is needed.

Of course, in a Christian context, as well as any medical help necessary to manage the symptoms, family and carers will want to be encouraging prayer ministry to find a long-term solution, but this needs to be approached with sensitivity. Remember, Jesus said to Bartimaeus, who was so obviously blind, "What do you want Me to do for you?" (Mark 10:51, NASB). The choices of the sufferer must always be respected.

However, very often, the faith and intercession of friends supporting the person suffering from depression will be vital in both starting and sustaining the journey of healing. Their unwavering belief in the certainty of God's ability to heal and their determination to support the person through the times of doubt cannot be underestimated. This is the Body of Christ in action.

Sometimes it is clear that the situation requires emergency intervention, particularly if the sufferer is thinking and talking about specific ways that they could commit suicide. Encouraging a depressed person to talk about their suicidal thoughts does not make them more likely to carry out this extreme action, but further professional help should be sought whenever ideas of "how to end it all" are being expressed in a more detailed way.

So, the journey of healing from depression will require much talking and much listening, both for the distress of the symptoms and when exploring any deeper traumas that may have been at the root of the problem. The story of Tamar, who was raped by her half-brother Amnon, reminds us that it is not just the trauma itself that deeply wounds us but perhaps, even more, an inability to express the injustice of that trauma. This can have a devasting effect on the well-being of a person's life.

> *2 Samuel 13:20... Then Absalom, her brother said to her, "Has Amnon your brother been with you? But now keep silent, my sister, he is your brother; do not take this matter to heart." So Tamar remained and was desolate in her brother Absalom's house.*
>
> *NASB*

The Hebrew word translated here as *desolate* comes from a root word meaning *numbness.* How well that describes the sense of emotional paralysis that is the experience of so many sufferers of depression. Tamar, in effect, had to shut down her feelings and not share them with anybody. Some translations of the verse actually refer to her condition as being *depressed.*

If only those around Tamar had been willing to really listen to her distress.

For this and the subsequent steps on the journey of healing, I will suggest a prayer that may help in reaching out to the Lord.

Sample prayer: *Father God, give me the courage to face the reality of the symptoms of depression that I am experiencing, and the courage to share this with those in the Body of Christ who can help me find God's way out of this desperate situation.*

[Recommended book: *Sarah* by Sarah Shaw, ISBN 9781852405113]

1. **The crossroads of believing that God has the way out of depression**

   Matthew 11:28... Come to Me, all who are weary and heavy-laden, and I will give you rest."

   NASB

This intersection on the journey simply requires a choice, but it's a tough choice, especially if there have been previous disappointments. It's not a choice based on feelings, but a decision to agree with the Word of God despite the current circumstances. Here are some important words of Jesus:

> *John 10:10... The thief comes only to steal and kill and destroy; I came that they may have life, and have it abundantly.*
>
> *NASB*

The symptoms of depression cannot be described as abundant life. Therefore, Jesus is declaring very powerfully here that one of the reasons He came onto this earth was to make it possible for people to be restored from the distress of a debilitating disorder like this. The journey may not be quick, but the destination is assured by Him.

Our friend Lucy, who sought the comfort of the pink blanket (in Chapter 2), remembers well the day that she was given the medical diagnosis of bipolar disorder. She recently explained how the label had seemed to be put upon her as something of a life-sentence. The doctor had not intended any harm to Lucy but his diagnosis and the negative expectations for her future were given with a powerful sense of authority. His words assumed that she would be subject to this disorder for the rest of her life, even though the symptoms could probably be significantly managed.

On her journey of healing, it became necessary for Lucy to speak out into the heavenly realms that she chose to believe that God would take her completely out of the condition of depression, not just help to alleviate the symptoms.

Sometimes the label of a diagnosis can even be a form of comfort, an identity which helps to validate feelings and coping behaviours. However, Lucy wanted God to define who she was, not the label of depression. She didn't know the route God would take her, but she chose to believe in His destination of freedom, in her identity as His child.

An important step for some will be to declare, or perhaps declare again, a choice for Jesus to be Lord of their lives, not least in the area of personal health. Trusting completely in Him marks a very significant step on a journey of hope, rather than a spiral of despair.

> *1 Peter 1:3... Praise be to the God and Father of our Lord Jesus Christ! In his great mercy he has given us new birth into a living hope through the resurrection of Jesus Christ from the dead.*
>
> *NIV*

Sample prayer: *Father God, despite times of disappointment, I choose to invite you afresh to be Lord of the whole of my life. I choose to believe that You have a way out for me from this dark place of depression. I believe You are completely faithful.*

2. **The crossroads of facing reality**

> *Psalm 139:23-24... Search me, O God, and know my heart; test me and know my anxious thoughts. See if there is any offensive way in me, and lead me in the way everlasting.*
>
> *NIV*

We need to bear in mind that a common symptom of depression is that we may not be able to think straight. We will probably need others to help us look at our situation with reality. For carers, this means sensitively encouraging the one who is suffering to be as real as possible about all that is going on, and to consider what might be triggering the problem or, more importantly, be at the root of the depression. There may be a need to help the person dismantle years of protective behaviours that have sought to hide the real issues, for example busyness at work, withdrawal into drink or drugs, or even the ability to hide behind laughter. It is well known that a significant number of professional comedians have struggled with serious bouts of depression behind the scenes.

> *Proverbs 14:13... Laughter may hide sadness. When happiness is gone, sorrow is always there.*
>
> *GNB*

Not thinking straight was certainly a significant issue for *our friend Derek*, the veterinary practitioner, who experienced his main period of depression as he was approaching retirement. Although he later realised that there were roots in a dysfunctional childhood, the doctors regarded the trigger at the time as nervous exhaustion. For some time, Derek had been trying to carry on doing a job (for which he says he was temperamentally unsuited) far beyond the point where his own resources could support him. He began to experience early waking, sometimes with tremors, digestive disorders, anxiety, persistent pessimism, social phobia, and eventually psychotic symptoms of distorted reality.

Derek described how he became irrationally convinced that he needed to continue working, specifically to fund the repair of a garden fence, which probably was only going to cost about £50! In fact, Derek's medical advisor referred to his condition as *impaired cognitive function*, and Derek was unable to understand clear advice from others or make good decisions for himself. Derek summed up how he had felt in these words:

> "In short, I was addled. I may have seemed OK to talk to, but the chances were that I was understanding and retaining only 5% or less of what I was hearing. I was confused."

But God was able to reach behind the confusion and despair. Unlike the time of his first experience of depression, Derek was now a committed Christian. He had come to know the continual leading and intervention of God, in the midst of the distressing symptoms. With the help of his wife and other believers, he sought God for the answers. As a young child, his home situation had been difficult, and Derek's way of coping had been to get away on his own for many hours at a time. In his present job he was experiencing queues of people at the door needing his attention, and there was no means of physical escape. Life had become utterly overwhelming. Derek recalled the process of restoration in these words:

> "Slowly the Lord led me up from the depths of my depressive state, where I had landed. He gave me pictures, snatch glimpses, mainly from childhood, of events which required forgiving of others, repentance, healing, or putting back under His authority. I gradually came back out of the depths. Today, I can testify to the healing power of prayer. I still have a bit to go but I have confidence, because of the road travelled thus far, that He will accomplish it in His time."

> *John 8:31-32... So Jesus said to those who believed in him, "If you obey my teaching, you are really my disciples; you will know the truth, and the truth will set you free.*
>
> *GNB*

Sample prayer: *Father, I recognise that I may not be able to see the issues at the heart this problem with sufficient clarity. I believe that You can show me the truth both directly and through those that You have provided to walk with me in Your way out of my depression.*

3. The crossroads of forgiving others

Mark 11:25… "Whenever you stand praying, forgive, if you have anything against anyone, so that Your Father who is in heaven will also forgive you your transgressions.

NASB

Dealing with the roots of depression will invariably require us to face often difficult issues of forgiving others. Some years ago, I had the privilege of praying with a young man (let's call him Simon) who had been experiencing times of deep depression, frequently lasting several days and recurring every few weeks. This young man was a fine Christian with a love of scripture that truly challenged me.

The bouts of despair found him sometimes crying for many hours and the situation was embarrassing for him and frustrating for the family. We talked about his life as a young boy and it became evident that, unbeknown to his father, he had been the object of serious bullying and abuse by many people. This included, in particular, one uncle with whom he had stayed for a while when his own family had been having some struggles. The uncle had treated him very badly, insulting him, locking him up for hours on end and lying to his parents about his behaviour. This had happened when he was five years old.

It's remarkable how often the Bible so accurately reflects the experiences of our lives today.

Psalm 69:20… Insults have broken my heart, and I am in despair. I had hoped for sympathy, but there was none; for comfort, but I found none.

GNB

We agreed that Simon had quite a long list of people to forgive. He decided to write down all the names (about 15) and one by one he spoke out forgiveness to each person whilst drawing a line through their names. He started with the easiest ones and as the list was gradually crossed out it was taking longer for each person. He took the act of forgiving each person very seriously and the process became more and more painful for him until there was only one name left on the list – the uncle. He took a long time to count the cost of forgiving that one person and during this time he scribbled more and more over the rest of the paper, leaving just the one name in a small white patch of paper.

Then, to my surprise, he suddenly said "God's telling me that if I don't forgive, it's like I'm working for the enemy." With that comment, he scribbled through the name and said, "I forgive him, so that's that."

I was taken aback by his straightforward manner. I fumbled through a few short prayers and asked God to answer the young man's cry for help. He then stood up and said, "It's done, I'm going swimming." Several weeks later I heard that the situation at home had improved dramatically. The times depression of had completely stopped.

This story of determination to walk God's way is different from the situation recently described to me by a Christian friend. Her older brother, who was not yet a believer, had been experiencing major depression for a long time, with many periods on medication. He had tried various talking-therapies, but these had had very limited success. He recognised that his family had a strong pattern of supressing emotions under a cloak of respectability and he had been carrying a lot of anger about situations that had occurred at school many years before. This had included the fact that the teachers had not realised he was dyslexic. His sister recalled with sadness recent words spoken to her by this troubled man, who was still unsure of God's love and ability to restore him:

> "I know one of the things they all say that I will have to do in order to get better: it's your thing – forgiveness – but I don't want to go there yet, I'm not ready for that."

Those we need to forgive are likely to include parents or others whose care for us has not been as God would have wanted, perhaps even abusive. For some, there will be those in the medical profession who have unwittingly made pronouncements over them or given them unhelpful labels.

I previously mentioned that when *our friend Lucy* heard her medical diagnosis of bipolar disorder, it sounded like a life-sentence. She felt no bitterness towards the doctor who had spoken to her in this way, but she knew that it was important for her to renounce the diagnosis as being unchangeable and to speak forgiveness to the doctor. Without knowing it, he had been the opportunity for the enemy to get a spiritual grip on her through that label.

Sometimes, as with Lucy's experience of someone speaking strongly over her life, we not only need to forgive them but we need to ask the Lord to release us from the ungodly ties that may continue to link us to them and to the words that they have spoken. These ties can give the powers of darkness an opportunity to lock us into the unhelpful words that have been spoken over our lives.

Sample prayer: *Father God, as I reflect on the wounding in my life that is at the root of this depression, I make a choice today to forgive all those who were the cause of that wounding. I forgive those who discouraged me from rightfully expressing my painful emotions. I also forgive those who have been unhelpful in their response to my bouts of depression by dismissing its significance or placing labels of diagnosis on me that have spiritually locked me into this disorder. Thank you that you can untie me from those who have had a negative effect on my life. I receive your freedom from these people and their unhelpful words.*

[Recommended books: *Forgiveness – God's Master Key* by Peter Horrobin, ISBN9781852405021 and *Soul Ties – the Unseen Bond in Relationships* by David Cross, ISBN 9781852405977]

4. **The crossroads of repentance**

   Psalm 32:3-5... When I kept silent, my bones wasted away through my groaning all day long. For day and night your hand was heavy upon me; my strength was sapped as in the heat of summer. Then I acknowledged my sin to you and did not cover up my iniquity. I said, "I will confess my transgressions to the Lord" – and you forgave the guilt of my sin.

   NIV

It's very hard to talk to someone, who has been struggling with depression, about the need to acknowledge any personal sin, when they are already facing a desperately difficult situation. However, the wounding that we have experienced in life frequently leads to our moving, often unconsciously, into sinful ways of trying to find resolution and comfort. In chapter 3, we looked, for example, at how the interaction between the soul and spirit within us can go out of line with God. When our soul tries to take a dominant lead in protecting the deep hurts in the spirit, we just end up further crushing ourselves on the inside rather than bringing protection and comfort.

When considering this issue some time ago, particularly in regard to the roots of depression, I felt the Lord point me to the following verses. God's people were pursuing their own ways of protecting the city of David in Jerusalem, without consulting Him. As a result, they ended up tearing down the very dwellings that the city wall was supposed to be protecting.

> *Isaiah 22:9-11...And you saw that the breaches in the wall of the city of David were many; and you collected the waters of the lower pool. Then you counted the houses of Jerusalem and tore down houses to fortify the wall. And you made a reservoir between the two walls for the waters of the old pool. But you did not depend on Him who made it, nor did you take into consideration Him who planned it long ago.*
>
> *NASB*

Our friend Peter grew up learning to be self-reliant in order to survive on the streets of a big city. Despite giving his life to Jesus as a boy, he became rebellious, distant from God and bitter about religion. He realises today that he was actively blocking God's love, for fear of disappointment, but thankfully Jesus never stopped searching for him.

At the age of 21, Peter suffered a smashed leg and a very severe head injury in a serious car accident. The prognosis was bad, with the possibility of becoming quadriplegic. However, very gradually, he did recover, and the pursuit of bodybuilding became the focus of his life, not only as an aid to recovery but as a means of finding the acceptance he craved, through a tough-guy identity.

Despite constant pain from the effects of the accident, he pushed himself to physical extremes, even taking up rugby, despite the advice of an orthopaedic consultant who said that he was forcing his body into a wheelchair. It wasn't long before this comment became a reality, and Peter found himself registered disabled, dependant on a walking stick, consuming 20 tablets a day in the form of painkillers and antidepressants and, indeed, often needing the aid of a wheelchair. In Peter's words: "I was once so strong in mind and body, and I couldn't believe what was happening to me."

One evening by a Scottish loch, several years later, following much trauma that included a devastating fire at the family home nearby, and a painful business failure, Peter fell to his knees in a place of utter brokenness.

> Before God, he acknowledged his pride, his reliance on his own intellect, stature, strength and ability, his imagined fearlessness, his damaging search for identity and not least his years of rejecting Jesus. As he wept, confessed and cried out to the Lord, a glimmer of hope came miraculously into his heart.

I'll conclude the story of Peter's healing a little later in this chapter, suffice it to say that the consequence of that repentance was nothing short of miraculous.

> *1 John 1:8-9... If we say that we have no sin, we deceive ourselves, and there is no truth in us. But if we confess our sins to God, he will keep his promise and do what is right: he will forgive us our sins and purify us from all our wrongdoing.*
>
> GNB

Sample prayer: *Father, I take full responsibility for the conscious and unconscious coping mechanisms that I have used in my life to hide away the pain and distress of inner wounding. I also confess the journey I have walked to seek healing from depression where this has not been Your way, and in fact has only added to the problem.*

5. **The crossroads of 'forgiving ourselves'**

> *Luke 15:18-19... "I will get up and go to my father, and will say to him, "Father, I have sinned against heaven, and in your sight; I am no longer worthy to be called your son; make me as one of your hired men."*
>
> NASB

Persistent and sometimes overwhelming feelings of guilt can be a major problem for some people experiencing bouts of depression. As he returned home, the prodigal son had trouble believing that he could be forgiven. In fact, he thought it necessary that he should continue to be punished for his rebellion, by being treated simply as an employee in his own family. But his father ran to him with a completely different agenda, an unconditional declaration that he was a loved, forgiven and valued son. This is exactly the attitude of our heavenly Father towards each one of us, as we come to him with a repentant heart.

I was reading an article recently on how to break free from the cycle of depression. The writer, who was not a Christian, described his downward spiral of destructive patterns of self-hate and self-punishment, and in his search for a solution he had come to the conclusion that, for him at least, …

> … self-forgiveness was one of the most powerful steps he needed to take on his quest for freedom. He realised that there had been so much anger directed in towards himself together with huge guilt concerning the many mistakes and failures of his life.

Sadly, he had no understanding of where to take his guilty feelings. He had nowhere to go to be assured of forgiveness. He had no source of true affirmation of his worth. For him, it all needed to be self-effort, and probably a lifetime of never-quite-fulfilled self-acceptance. He had a part of the answer to his battle with depression, but he hadn't found the One who could be his assurance of victory.

For a follower of Jesus there is somewhere to take the guilty feelings and a certainty that God's forgiveness is absolute. We no longer have to walk with the weight of guilt. The enemy would want us to carry this burden, pressuring us to doubt the amazing truth that there is no requirement for us to endure further punishment. Forgiving ourselves is perhaps better expressed as an agreement with God that, through repentance of sin, we are completely released from every debt that may have been due. God's forgiveness needs to be fully received in order to be effective in restoring inner peace.

Colossians 2:14... Having cancelled out the certificate of debt consisting of decrees against us, which was hostile to us; and He has taken it out of the way, having nailed it to a cross.
NASB

Sample prayer: *Father, I've carried a lot of guilt and shame from the mistakes of the past, and even false guilt through the stigma associated with depression. I choose to say that, as You have forgiven me for all the things that I have got wrong, I now stand in agreement with You and declare that I am fully forgiven, and all the debt has been paid. I forgive myself!*

6. **The crossroads of dealing with false guilt and shame**
   Isaiah 61:7a... Instead of their shame my people will receive a double portion, and instead of disgrace they will rejoice in their inheritance. NIV

Our friend Lucy found that during her walk into God's healing from depression, shame was always a dominant issue. Firstly, there was the shame she felt, as a Christian, for even having a problem with depression and being on medication for so many years. Gradually God brought her to a place of recognising that this shame was not the consequence of her sinful actions but rather a work of condemnation by the enemy. She was able to resolve this with the Lord, but the greater issue was the realisation that she had been carrying, from the earliest moments of her life, a huge burden of family shame.

Lucy's father had been an alcoholic, causing immense disorder in the family, and her mother had been completely unable to deal with the situation. Lucy realised that she had unconsciously taken on the role of hiding the family dysfunction from the rest of the world. At the same time she had been trying to calm her father's drunken moods, while seeking to be as perfect a little girl as possible in order to somehow counteract the behaviour of her damaged parents. The more she took on these responsibilities, the more she seemed to carry the family shame, particularly when embarrassing issues became public knowledge.

Lucy began to realise that this shame-carrying and false responsibility had been a pattern of her life into adulthood and into her marriage. As she looked at her forebears, she also realised that there had been significant shame issues in the family connected with adultery, psychiatric problems and suicide. It became apparent to her that a burden of inherited shame, something that was not the consequence of her own sin, had been given a huge opportunity to cloak her life.

As she chose to shed this cloak, with the help of the Lord, there was a powerful opportunity for God's healing and release from a weight that had burdened her spirit for so many years.

Sample prayer: *Father, You have created feelings of shame to help us realise the spiritual exposure in our lives when we have sinned. But I have felt shame for situations that are not my fault. I choose to remove this cloak of shame that doesn't belong to me and release it to be carried, where appropriate, by those who should be doing so.*

7. **The crossroads of asking God to cleanse our spiritual inheritance**

   1 Peter 1:18-19... For you know what was paid to set you free from the worthless manner of life handed down by your ancestors. It was not something that can be destroyed, such as silver or gold; it was the costly sacrifice of Christ, who was like a lamb without defect or flaw.

GNB

Jack is a dear Christian brother. Some time ago, when he had been a believer for about ten years, he heard some teaching on the negative consequences that the sinful practices of our ancestors can have on our own lives today. He was in a place on his Christian journey where he knew that his walk with Jesus lacked the freedom that he saw in other people, freedom to experience the gifts of the Holy Spirit and freedom to move beyond religion into a true relationship with God. To put it simply, his Christian walk was dark and heavy.

He knew that on both his father's and his mother's side of the family there had been involvement with the Orange Order. This is a religious organisation, particularly found in Northern Ireland and very similar to Freemasonry. Its tenets are not consistent with biblical Christianity.

During a time of prayer ministry, Jack decided to speak out forgiveness to those in his family line who had been in the Orange Order and had, by their involvement, brought a defiled spiritual inheritance into his own life. Jack recalls being very surprised when he found himself going through clear deliverance, something he'd never experienced before, and he knew in that moment that something of religious heaviness had been removed.

Within a matter of days Jack found himself embarking on a whole new pathway of Holy Spirit anointing and gifting, a walk with Jesus that was, for the first time, filled with vision and colour. Jack would not have described himself as having been *depressed* but he knew for certain that he had been *oppressed* by a demonically empowered spiritual inheritance, that God had supernaturally cleansed.

Sometimes we also need to acknowledge negative traits in our lives that have come from a spiritual inheritance that has affected the nation to which we belong. On occasions, when praying with Scottish or Jewish people, for example, there have been strong issues of rejection spiritually embedded in their lives, resulting from events in the history of those nations. In Nordic countries, there is an entrenched belief system, referred to as the *Law of Jante* which has clearly affected the vitality of many lives, albeit unconsciously. The philosophy embraced by this law, or code of conduct, strongly opposes individual worth and achievement.

These are just brief examples of a national spiritual legacy that can sometimes feed the other roots of depression in our lives. Followers of Jesus are, of course, citizens of many precious nations, but our spiritual citizenship now lies in a new Kingdom where our value and acceptance are undisputed.

Jesus has bought us redemption from any defiled inheritance handed down from our ancestors by His shedding of blood on the Cross. However, as with all aspects of the healing ministry of Jesus, it's important for us to acknowledge those specific areas of our lives that need His touch. We personally need to lay hold of what has been fulfilled at the Cross.

Sample prayer: *Father, I recognise that some of the disorder in my life was rooted in the sinful beliefs and behaviours of my family and* *national forebears. I forgive them for the effect that their life-choices have had in my life, and I receive the full redemption, purchased by Jesus at the Cross, for cleansing of this defiled spiritual inheritance, particularly in relation to depression.*

[Recommended book: *It Isn't Free and It Isn't Masonry* by Otto Bixler, ISBN 9781852408701]

8. **The crossroads of letting God be our Defender**
   Psalm 27:1... The Lord is my light and my salvation; Whom shall I fear? The Lord is the defence of my life; Whom shall I dread?

   NASB

The disordered interaction between the human soul and the human spirit is, I suggest, a key issue at the root of much of the depression with which so many people struggle. We have looked at soulish self-protection, the unconscious inner choices which override God's ways of guarding the sensitive, and perhaps wounded, human spirit within us. I have suggested that this can be like pulling down the houses of a city in order to build up the outer defences, creating devastation to the very thing that we are seeking to protect. The people of Jerusalem did exactly that:

> *Isaiah 22:10b-11a... [You] tore down houses to fortify the wall... but you did not depend on Him who made it.*
>
> *NASB*

We can hear God's heart-cry, saying, "Why did you not come to Me to find the protection you sought? I am Creator of this world and I know how to make it safe for you." For many people, the years of protective behaviour have often resulted in any hurting place within us being a deeply hidden, if not completely abandoned, and a very dark part of our being. The solution today is to confess our wrongful coping and defence mechanisms, sometimes needing to do this even before we have fully understood how they have operated.

Sample prayer: *Father God, my own internal defence mechanisms have not worked. Indeed, they have probably done me more harm than good. I make a choice today to let You be the guard over my spirit, showing me which ways of behaviour, and which people, are safe or unsafe. Forgive me and cleanse me from the years of soulish self-protection.*

9. **The crossroads of letting God touch our heart**

   Isaiah 61:3a... [The Lord has anointed Me to] provide for those who grieve in Zion – to bestow on them a crown of beauty instead of ashes, the oil of gladness instead of mourning, and a garment of praise instead of a spirit of despair.

   NIV

   Matthew 5:3... Blessed are the poor in spirit, for theirs is the kingdom of heaven.

   NASB

As we have seen, our natural tendency throughout life is to suppress the distress in our hearts by trying, in our own strength, to cope with, dissociate from, or defend, the deep and painful place within. It is this very place within us that is likely to hold the key to the roots of depression, so it is vital that we give God the opportunity to reach into that place with His reality and His healing.

It is important that we give God permission to reach into territory that we have tried to keep *under a blanket,* hidden from everyone, including from Him. It's time to let light into that hidden place in our human spirit. Incidentally, concealing our pain has just created an opportunity for the enemy to hold a part of us in his darkness.

> *Psalm 143:3-4... The enemy pursues me, he crushes me to the ground; he makes me dwell in darkness like those long dead. So my spirit grows faint within me; my heart within me is dismayed.*
>
> *NIV*

Jesus is ready to call us out of that place, like the way He called Lazarus out of the grave. Our soulish control has very often had the effect of binding up our spirit, at least in part, in a tomb of lifelessness. Now is a precious opportunity to respond to His call.

> *John 11:43-44... When He [Jesus] had said these things, He cried out with a loud voice, "Lazarus, come forth." The man who had died came forth, bound hand and foot with wrappings, and his face was wrapped around with a cloth. Jesus said to them, "Unbind him, and let him go."*
>
> *NASB*

Let me describe the story of *our friend Amy.* She believes that the pivotal moment on her journey of healing was when, in her words, "I learned to talk about things and realised that there's nothing wrong with crying." As a little girl of seven, as a result of family dysfunction, she had cried herself to sleep most nights. However, when her parents told her that expressing emotions was selfish and wrong, she made a choice to suppress the overwhelming grief that had gripped her life.

Her disabled brother, for whom she had been made responsible despite her young age, had been taken into a care home. Amy was convinced that, if she had done a better job of caring for him, he wouldn't have had to leave home. She was devasted by this loss and there was no comfort from her mother, who was not only involved in witchcraft but made it very clear to Amy that she was an unwanted burden.

Amy's suppression of grief was pursued through over-eating, reading fantasy books, studying hard at school and, later as a teenager, just trying not to be noticed by those around her. In fact, at times of extreme despair, she remembers wishing that she had been dead. Then at the age of seventeen, she accepted Jesus as her Lord and Saviour. Despite the fact that for the first time she realised she was loved by Someone, the depression continued to affect her life, curtailing her time at university. She had made an unconscious decision that no one was allowed to touch the deep hurting place, not even God.

There followed marriage, Christian work in Israel, bouts of post-natal depression after the birth of each of her four children, a time at a Bible college and then, quite suddenly, a mental breakdown and admission into a psychiatric hospital. As Amy describes it: "I could not cope any longer with trying to be a good Christian." Then one day a Christian doctor, who had prescribed anti-depressants, explained to her the true meaning of forgiveness.

She had firmly believed throughout her life that, as a good Christian, forgiveness meant that she should pretend that all the things that had deeply hurt her should be thought of as if they had never really happened. Now, at last, she was able to overcome the fear of talking about the deep hurts and allow herself to cry when she felt the pain. This became the start of a radical healing process.

Amy has been off antidepressants for fifteen years. Although she describes herself as occasionally feeling 'a bit wobbly', she now has the biblical tools to help her with any of the old feelings that arise, feelings such as being useless, unwanted or unmotivated. She says that she now has a certainty of God's purposes in her life and can quickly deal with any forgiveness issues, any unhealthy boundaries or wrong ties in relationships. Most of all, she has learned to be able to share her deep thoughts with others and with God whenever the need arises. God has truly restored her!

Being able to voice the deep concerns of the heart, both to God directly and to other trusted members of the Body of Christ, is an essential step on the journey of healing from depression. Sometimes we don't know precisely what those deep feelings are because that part of our lives has been abandoned for so long. One of the reasons that God has given His children the gift of tongues is for us to be able to express heart issues that are difficult to put into words. The Holy Spirit is there to help us voice these deep concerns.

> *Romans 8:26... In the same way, the Spirit helps us in our weakness. We do not know what we ought to pray for. But the Spirit Himself intercedes for us with groans that words cannot express.*
>
> *NIV*

Expressing thoughts to and through Him, using simple creativity, can also bring a similar benefit in the healing process. Both the use of tongues and creative pursuits engage our human spirit, in some measure. These open a door to the leading of the Holy Spirit, giving Him the opportunity to bring revelation, healing and direction, so that we have an antidote to our natural soulish control. We will look a little more at the significant tool of creativity in the next chapter. However, it's important to mention here that it is a childlike willingness to engage in creative activities that God is most able to use, rather than our pursuing perfect artistic results.

> *Our friend Annie*, the lady who had such a struggle with treatments such as ECT, said recently that simple creativity had been an indispensable tool in her journey of healing from depression. She described how creative activity had allowed the Holy Spirit to bypass all the defences and blockages that she had unconsciously developed in her mind, in trying to protect herself from further hurt in the damaged places within.

Sample prayer: *Father, the symptoms of my depression point to damage in my human spirit. Show me how I can best open my heart to Your touch of revelation and healing in the core of my being. I* *choose to remove any barriers that I have erected in the past, in trying to hide this hurting, but precious, part of my being.*

10. **The crossroads of finding assurance of our true identity in Christ**
    Romans 8:15-16... For you have not received a spirit of slavery leading to fear again, but you have received a spirit of adoption as sons by which we cry out, "Abba! Father!" The Spirit Himself testifies with our spirit that we are children of God."

    NASB

It's often said that the main problem we have today is that we are struggling with an identity crisis. The media promotes an ever-changing ideal image and, the fact is, the vast majority of us just don't match up! Many of us need to reassess who or what is going to define the person we are; do we allow public opinion to define us or do we let the unchanging Word of God have that rule over our lives? Whatever the world chooses to say about you, your worth to God has been proved by the payment of His Son's life; you are that valuable!

It's important to restate here that depression is not just a mood disorder but, more significantly, it is an identity disorder. Indeed, it has rightly been described as an identity thief. It's time for us to claim back what belongs to every follower of Jesus.

We have been restored into our true God-given identity as one of His treasured children, the certainty of a place in His family. The world may well have tried to put labels on us such as failure, misfit, no-hoper, outsider, but we do not belong to this world now. We may well have put labels on ourselves, with statements such as *I'll always be a depressive,* but the experiences of life do not need to define our identity.

The story of Mephibosheth gives us an extraordinary insight into the link between trauma, identity and despair. At the age of five, following the death of his father and grandfather, while he and his nurse were fleeing for safety, Mephibosheth fell and became crippled in both feet. While living in an insignificant place called Lo-debar, he was called to the palace by King David, in order to fulfil a covenant promise made by the king to Mephibosheth's father Jonathan. David clearly wanted to give him a special position of value in the royal household, but from deep within Mephibosheth's heart came words that spoke of inner despair and a sense of worthlessness:

> *2 Samuel 9:8… Again he prostrated himself and said, "What is your servant, that you should regard a dead dog like me?"*
> *NASB*

In just the same way, the King of kings beckons us today to come and join His royal household irrespective of the ways that we have been regarded by ourselves or by others in the past. Depression does indeed give opportunity for the enemy to be an identity thief. Part of the journey of healing is not only to recognise this issue but to confront the attempted robbery of our God-ordained and significant position in His family. Jesus has promised that He will not leave His followers in a spiritually abandoned, fatherless condition, which is such a common feeling for those struggling with depression.

John 14:18... I will not leave you as orphans; I will come to you.

NASB

Sample prayer: *Father, I know that the enemy would like to steal my God-ordained identity by putting labels upon me of being a hopeless case, a depressive or a failure. These and other names may have described something of my experiences in life, but they do not define who I am. I choose today to stand in the identity that You have given me, a precious child of God, walking with You into my healing.*

[Recommended book: *Loved Like Never Before* by Ken Symington, ISBN 9781852405854]

11. **The crossroads of expelling the enemy**
    Acts 10:38... "You know of Jesus of Nazareth, how God anointed Him with the Holy Spirit and with power, and how He went about doing good and healing all were oppressed by the devil, for God was with Him."

    NASB

Spiritual oppression from the enemy can feed the roots of depression, if he is given the opportunity. We looked in the last chapter at how personal or family involvement in false religion or the occult can be an opening for the powers of darkness to get a grip on our lives and promote inner disorder such as depression. Jesus was familiar with the affliction of the enemy, but He refused to let it grip Him, as he carefully walked in the will of His Father. As we walk with Jesus, we can know release from that grip with which the evil one seeks to establish his control in our lives.

> *Isaiah 53:7-8... He was oppressed and afflicted, yet he did not open his mouth; he was led like a lamb to the slaughter, and as a sheep before her shearers is silent, so he did not open his mouth. By oppression and judgement he was carried away. And who can speak of his descendants? For he was cut off from the land of the living; for the transgression of my people he was stricken.*
> NIV

Some years ago, my wife and I had the privilege of praying with *our friend Anthony*, a lovely pastor who was struggling with bouts of depression. There were several issues that were contributing to the problem but one of them I remember very well. He had been brought up in a loving family home but both parents had been involved in spiritualism, seeking to communicate with the spiritual realm in order to find some measure of peace in their lives.

Anthony had not been directly involved but because there had been spiritualist meetings in the family home there was, in his memory, an oppressive feeling within the house. Any exploration into the spiritual realms, outside of the authority and protection of Jesus, is dangerous territory. Therefore, Anthony's parents had unwittingly given invitation to the powers of darkness to defile their home.

As we prayed with Anthony, he forgave his parents for allowing this spiritual exposure of his life. We asked the Lord to release him from the oppressive powers that had been in the house, and to remove from him whatever was still holding a place of darkness within him. "Wow, I can feel it leaving," he said, "I had no idea that I had been carrying that with me all this time."

It was not the end of Anthony's search for freedom from depression, but it was clearly a significant step for him to be rid of that particular hold and defilement by the powers of darkness. We ourselves, or those who have carried any spiritual responsibility for our lives, give the enemy opportunity to oppress us when lifestyle choices are made that are in rebellion to the ways of God. Thankfully, He has made a way for our deliverance through the defeat of the enemy at the Cross, and we take hold of that victory by extending forgiveness to others and by receiving God's forgiveness for ourselves.

When there is disorder in our soul and spirit, perhaps rooted in neglect, abuse or trauma, and it has been exacerbated by our own attempts to fix the problem, this disorder can give the enemy an opportunity to have some control. For example, scripture is clear that although anger is a right response to injustice, burying that anger, for whatever reason, is not just unhelpful, but can give a foothold for demonic activity. This can be true even in the life of a Christian. Let's remind ourselves again of what Paul says to the members of the church in Ephesus.

> *Ephesians 4:26-27… "In your anger do not sin": Do not let the sun go down while you are still angry, and do not give the devil a foothold.*
>
> *NIV*

The powers of darkness do not initiate the symptoms of depression, but they can strengthen it, through spiritual intrusion and oppression, by taking advantage of any aspect of our lives that has become out of line with God's created order. Truth always exposes the works of the enemy, while forgiveness takes away his rights to grip our lives. The enemy cannot possess the life of one of God's children, but he can have a measure of spiritual authority if given the opportunity. In the following verse, Paul describes this situation as Satan *getting the upper hand* where, for example, someone continues in unforgiveness.

> *2 Corinthians 2:10-11... When you forgive someone for what he has done, I forgive him too. For when I forgive – if, indeed, I need to forgive anything – I do it in Christ's presence because of you, in order to keep Satan from getting the upper hand of us; for we know what his plans are.*
>
> *GNB*

[Recommended book: *Healing Through Deliverance* by Peter Horrobin, ISBN 9781852404987]

Sample command to the powers of darkness: *Enemy, through these prayers to the Living God, through the forgiveness both given and received, the license previously handed to you is removed. Your authority to drive parts of my life into destructive cycles is finished. In the name of Jesus, I command every power of darkness promoting the issues around depression to leave my whole being now, for it is to the Holy Spirit of God that I give control of my life this day.*

12. **The crossroads of physical healing**

    Proverbs 17:22... A joyful heart is good medicine, but a broken spirit dries up the bones.

    NASB

Medical practice back in the Middle Ages recognised the link between the spiritual and physical condition of those suffering with disease. In fact, early hospitals were part of church premises, seeking to serve both the temporal and spiritual needs of the patient. Modern medicine has seen amazing advances in treatment but has lost understanding of the interaction of the body, soul and spirit. Even psychiatry and the cure of physical disease have been treated as largely separate disciplines until relatively recently.

According to the Bible, the biology and chemistry of the physical body will always, to some extent, reflect the condition of the soul and spirit. When there is an electrical problem inside a computer the consequence is usually very evident on the screen. In a similar way, emotional and spiritual damage within our own bodies will inevitably reveal itself in physical symptoms. The good news is that, as God restores the inner broken places and delivers us from the holds of the enemy, we can also come to Him seeking repair to any associated effects in the body. Examples of this can include a sleep problem, headaches, immune system disorder and heart disease.

Let me conclude the story of *our friend Peter* that I started earlier in this chapter, returning to the day when God met him by the side of a Scottish loch. From that moment of repentance everything changed, despite many hard challenges on the subsequent journey. Step by step, over a number of years, Peter has been able to give up dependence on a walking stick, stop the anti-depressants and gradually reduce the painkillers. In addition, he has found physical healing from the effects of traumas of the past, been able to give up the government's long-term incapacity benefit and overcome deep issues of shame. Lastly, and probably the most special for him, he has become well-established in work again as a self-employed handyman.

Here are Peter's own words: "The cost for me of my healing has been to surrender my life to God. He has truly restored the years that locusts had eaten, and He now uses me to teach others about the effects of sin and the reality of the spiritual battle. God reminded me recently that I'm still a body-builder but now it's for building up the Body of Christ!"

Sample prayer: *Father God, as you bind up my broken heart and set this captive free from spiritual oppression, I come to You for healing of this precious temple of Your Holy Spirit, my body. Restore Your divine order in the flow of neurotransmitters, in the functioning of my immune system and in all the chemistry of my body. I ask for restoration of my sleep patterns, appetite and heart rhythms to be in line with Your divine order for my body.*

Key points from this chapter

- God's healing from depression is a journey which comprises significant moments of His revelation, vital moments of our decision in how to respond, and the extraordinary moments of His supernatural restoration.

- His roadmap of healing will be different for each person but there will be similar intersections or crossroads along the way.

- These crossroads, to which God will direct us, in whatever order He chooses, are likely to include some, or perhaps all, of the following:

  Sharing the problem with God and with trusted friends. Facing the truth of the symptoms, the triggers and the possible causes.

  Making a choice to believe that God really does have a way out of the depression, as we seek to follow Him.

  Recognising that God alone knows the full reality of our lives and that, as we receive and act on the revelation He gives, the opportunity for freedom will come.

  Forgiving those who have been responsible for the deep wounding of our lives, and also those who have been uncaring or unhelpful in our walk out of depression.

  Repenting of the life-choices that have been harmful to us, often the attempts, even if subconscious, to try and disconnect from the true feelings of hurt and distress in our hearts.

  Forgiving ourselves, in agreement with God, for the ways in which we have inadvertently harmed ourselves, often while trying to suppress pain.

  Giving God any false guilt or shame that others have placed on us, or where perhaps we have wrongly assumed it was our responsibility to carry it for the family to which we belonged.

Dealing with any spiritual inheritance that has made us predisposed to the symptoms of depression.

Making a choice to trust God to be the Defender and the Provider of our lives, giving up our long-established coping mechanisms.

Allowing God access and opportunity to bring His restoration to the damage in the human spirit.

Finding God's assurance of our true identity in Him, as beloved children of our Heavenly Father.

Driving out the powers of darkness that have been given opportunity to promote the disorder of depression.

Seeking God for physical healing

CHAPTER 6

Some practical suggestions

Getting active in our choices

Alongside a prayer journey of restoration with the Lord, which I have outlined in the last chapter, many who have walked out of the grip of depression have found considerable help in pursuing activities of a more practical nature. This attention to lifestyle choices was certainly adopted by many of those who have given testimony in this book. In fact, the suggestions in this chapter should not be considered as less important in our walk of healing than the times of prayer. They encourage Godly ways of living and some of the activities give an excellent opportunity for the Lord to speak to us. This can perhaps be in situations where we are less focussed on the day-to-day struggle with the symptoms of depression.

Healing through creativity

It is well known that Winston Churchill, when struggling with his 'black dog' of depression, frequently turned to painting in order to find a measure of relief. But creative pursuits can have a much more important role on the pathway out of depression than just providing helpful solace. They can be an opportunity for the inner voice of our spirit, prompted by the Lord, to be heard through the vehicle of creative expression. For example, it can be a time for an important surfacing of unrealised fears, guilt or shame, or perhaps we will experience unexpected tears or laughter, or we may recognise the pressure of perfectionism. It can truly be an opportunity to find ourselves in a new way.

For many people, it has been a breakthrough experience when they encounter their inner troubled self, under the direction of the Holy Spirit. It has proved to be an opportunity to recognise the roots of their struggles with depression. The creative activity needs to be as free from the constraints of performance as possible, free to make mistakes and reflect on what might be being revealed through even our imperfect efforts. From experience at our ministry centres, one of the most effective activities has been what we have called *messy painting*, where the guest, dressed in suitable protective clothing, is able to fully engage with the paints, on big sheets of paper, without the need to worry about how messy they get! The aim is to facilitate connection to something of self that has been lost along life's journey, and to connect with God, not to create an artistic masterpiece.

Under God's leading, many kinds of creativity can be of value in discovering more of ourselves: pottery, woodwork, making jewellery, drama, singing and banner-making, for example. Again, it should be emphasised that it is not so much the result that usually touches the heart but the process. It's important to welcome the Holy Spirit into the experience and listen to your own inner desires about what to do or to make. Then, be open to Him bringing revelation of what are the true attitudes of your heart, whether good or bad. Although God certainly responds when we are alone, there is something very special about doing this in a spiritually safe environment alongside reliable Christian brothers and sisters. The family of God can encourage and share in what God is saying or doing.

God is the Creator of the universe and we are all made in His image, so there is a creative dimension within us all, rooted in our human spirit. Some may be gifted with particular skills, but we are all creative and, as we enter into creative activities with Him, He works powerfully to bring connection to our own self and to Him.

> *Psalm 90:17... May the favour of the Lord our God rest upon us; establish the work of our hands for us – yes, establish the work of our hands.*
>
> *NIV*

[Recommended book: *Healing Through Creativity* by Fiona Horrobin, ISBN 978-1-852408-37-4]

Food for the spirit, soul and body

We have been looking in depth at the needs of our soul and spirit, but how should we best feed the body to aid us in the journey of recovery? Jesus encouraged His followers to ask God for our daily food, to provide all that is necessary to sustain us, not least physically and emotionally. Healthy eating is very unlikely to be the only answer in seeking relief from major depression, but we should not ignore the fact that God has given the medical profession an understanding of what are sometimes referred to as *good mood foods*. A poor diet is likely to be high in sugars, processed foods and bad fats (trans-fats). A good diet is likely to contain balanced quantities of vegetables, lean meat, fruit and good fats (from fish oils, and nuts).

Without letting healthy food become an obsessive pursuit, the right nutrients clearly do have an influence on our mood. Examples of this would be a balanced intake of olive oil, ginger, cinnamon, tomatoes, fish, apples, berries and nuts (almonds, cashews and walnuts), pumpkin seeds, squash, sweet potatoes and turmeric. All these get a "thumbs-up" in good-food guides connected with advice on anxiety issues and mood disorders.

Interestingly, a number of these foods are considered to have natural anti-inflammatory properties. This means that they can chemically counteract the chronic responses of the immune system mentioned in a previous chapter, those responses which are frequently linked to depression. Of course, these foods can help manage the chemical condition of the body, but they do not solve the root issue of why the body feels the need to remain in a defensive posture. Those "instructions" are very likely to be coming from the unresolved issues of the heart.

"Let there be light"

These are words found in the first few verses of the Bible, followed by this significant statement: "God saw that the light was good," (Genesis 1:3-4). There has been important secular research during the last few decades into the effects of light and dark on the functioning of the human body. The clear conclusion is that the human body significantly benefits from natural light. It's interesting to note that, even on an overcast day, the level of light outside our houses is roughly ten times the level within.

For many years it's been known that there is a clear connection between the functioning of the body and the amount of received light during the day. It has been understood that sunlight is necessary for the production of vitamin D in our bodies, but it also seems that light positively affects our immune system, our blood pressure and, not least, our body-clocks. This twenty-four-hour cycle of chemical activity is called the *circadian rhythm* of our bodies. Furthermore, there is growing evidence that a morning walk in daylight, for example, can have a measurable curative effect on disorders such as depression. This level of light early in the day strengthens the circadian cycle, whereas strong light late at night can disrupt these body rhythms and damage sleep patterns. So, spending a lot of time on electronic devices before bed is not helpful for our well-being.

It is known that early January, at least in the Northern Hemisphere, is a time when doctors see a peak in cases of depression. S.A.D., seasonal affective disorder, is sometimes known as winter depression because its symptoms are more apparent and more severe during the winter. It is very likely that this disorder results from lower levels of natural light during the winter months. Besides walking in daylight, some have found that the use of a light-therapy box can be helpful, and this was certainly true for *our friend Derek*, as part of his practical steps to healing. There are many brands of light box on the market, so it's best to do some careful research and comparison before purchase. It would be good to ask the Lord if this extra provision of light, even from an electrical device, might be of help to the daily rhythms that He has designed for the body. This might be especially useful for those unable to exercise outside.

The benefits of exercise

Eric Liddell, whose story was shown in the film *Chariots of Fire*, once said, "God made me fast and when I run, I can feel His pleasure." Now, we don't all have to be as athletic as Mr Liddell, but God clearly intended our bodies to enjoy exercise and to benefit from it. He designed every part of our being to function in a certain way, for us to use our body each day to carry out His purposes. Adam and Eve were expected to physically tend God's creation in the Garden of Eden which, no doubt, would have been very demanding yet very satisfying work!

Depression, inactivity and heart disease form an unhealthy interactive alliance, both affecting and being affected by each other. People with depression have a slower recovery after an acute heart event, and research has shown that those who were physically inactive before cardiac surgery were significantly more likely to have symptoms of depression both before and after the surgery.

Many people have found that exercise helps mediate stress, anxiety and depression, raising the levels of serotonin and dopamine in the brain, especially when the exercise is outside in the daylight. It could be a very important part of your healing journey to make the decision to take a brisk walk each day, if possible, of at least twenty minutes, an opportunity for your body to experience the benefits of both exercise and natural light. If you are able, a *stroll* in God's creation would often be much better for you than a *scroll* on a Facebook page!

Develop an attitude of gratitude

Gratitude has been described as the purest form of all positive emotions. There has been significant research[(b)] into the effects of a lifestyle of thankfulness on personal well-being. The results have been extraordinary, apparently with conclusive proof that a thankful heart has a substantial and positive effect on mood, the immune system, blood pressure and cardiac functioning.

Expressions of gratitude need a direction, someone to thank. This can of course be other people, but for Christians we have the ultimate focus for our thankfulness, the One who most cares for us. G. K. Chesterton, the writer, once said, "The worst moment for an atheist is when he is really thankful and has no-one to thank." We shouldn't be surprised that the Bible gives some very clear advice on the practice and benefits of thankfulness:

> *Philippians 4:6-7… Be anxious for nothing, but in everything by prayer and supplication with thanksgiving let your requests be made known to God. And the peace of God, which surpasses all comprehension, will guard your hearts and your minds in Christ Jesus.*
>
> *NASB*

(b) "The Neuroscience of Gratitude and How it Affects Anxiety and Grief". Madhulegna Roy Chowdhury 2019

This passage tells us that approaching God with a thankful heart will have a very positive effect on our minds, an effect well beyond human understanding. There is something spiritually powerful about gratitude that opens a pathway to God's intervention in our lives. The passage in Philippians goes on to encourage us to dwell on the good things of life.

> *Philippians 4:8… Finally, brethren, whatever is true, whatever is honourable, whatever is right, whatever is pure, whatever is lovely, whatever is of good repute, if there is any excellence and if anything is worthy of praise, dwell on these things.*
>
> *NASB*

Praise is almost synonymous with thankfulness. We are being encouraged here to walk in a lifestyle of celebrating and applauding everything and everyone that daily benefits our lives. An attitude of gratitude can truly be life changing. The Bible and mental health research are in agreement! Some have labelled gratitude as a natural antidepressant because it helps to release dopamine, serotonin and other neurotransmitters which are responsible for mood enhancement. Apparently, it also results in a marked reduction in cortisol, the stress hormone, and it triggers "good" hormones which positively affect the functioning of the immune system.

So, how do we take advantage of these secular and biblical truths about thankfulness? Here are some suggestions, for followers of Jesus:

- Irrespective of feelings, keep a daily journal, addressed to God, of those things for which you can give thanks (1 Thessalonians 5:18).

- List those people who have been, or currently are, a source of benefit to your life. If possible, send some of those people a note of thanks.
- Thank God specifically for His daily provision and protection.
- Thank Him for all the ways your body has served you well, even if some parts of your body are currently not working so well.
- Agree with Him that you are wonderfully made (Psalm 139:14).
- Read aloud Psalm 100.
- Share these thoughts of thankfulness with a trusted and prayerful friend.

Look for ways to de-stress your life

Proverbs 12:25a… Anxiety in a man's heart weighs it down…
NASB

God's desire is to lead us out of depression but it's important to recognise our part in caring for the body that He has given us during our time on earth. Stress is part of life, heightening the functions of the body in order to deal with day to day issues. However, our life-choices can unnecessarily add to that stress which, although unlikely to be the cause of depression, can certainly trigger the underlying vulnerability, and worsen the symptoms of a depressive episode.

Perhaps this is a good opportunity to look at your job, your relationships, your responsibilities, your church commitments, your leisure time. Bringing these before the Lord and reassessing what is His will in each of these areas can have a significant effect on the levels of stress that you are experiencing. He certainly has no intention of overloading you beyond the spiritual, emotional and physical strength that He has provided.

Stress and anxiety go hand in hand, and the Bible frequently encourages us to avoid anxiety by making a decision to trust God at a deeper level, expecting Him to provide our needs and protect us from harm. In fact, a lifestyle of anxiety or worry can even be regarded as a choice to disobey a command of God. There's never any condemnation from Him but, for our wellbeing, it's good to be reminded of these important words from Jesus:

> *Matthew 6:25-34… "Therefore I tell you, do not worry about your life… Who of you by worrying can add a single hour to his life?… So do not worry, saying, 'What shall we eat?' or 'What shall we drink?' or 'What shall we wear?'… Therefore do not worry about tomorrow…"*
>
> *NIV*

Be careful where you go for help

The pathway to healing that Jesus offers each one of us is there to bring us into abundant life. Depression is the antithesis of that abundance. There are many therapies that offer renewed vitality and vigour, and they are certainly not all bad, but we need to be very careful with those that have a spiritual dimension to the treatment. There is an enemy who is only too ready to seduce us into his solution for our troubled lives, but he is a thief.

> *John 10:10... "The thief comes only to steal and kill and destroy; I [Jesus] came that they may have life, and have it abundantly."*
>
> *NASB*

Any holistic remedy or therapy seeking to restore our spiritual condition must be considered spiritually suspect if it is not consistent with the teaching of Jesus and therefore governed by His spiritual authority. According to the Bible, there can be no true spiritual restoration without the resolution of sin, through our confession and God's forgiveness. I have not personally found one alternative therapy that deals with sin so, for a follower of Jesus, looking to these therapies for spiritual healing is a mistake. Jesus provides the only solution to any spiritual disorder within our bodies. No amount of holistic treatment in spiritual "re-balancing", "unblocking", "harmonising" or "energy transfer" will ever meet the need. Even when a label such as *Christian Aromatherapy* is added to the practice, it cannot replace the essential step of receiving God's forgiveness for our spiritual repair.

Let's look at yoga, for example. This meditative practice is increasingly being promoted by the medical profession as a helpful tool in destressing our lives, but that was not the purpose of this practice in its Hindu and Buddhist origins. The postures of yoga were designed in order to make the body increasingly receptive to the spiritual powers being invoked in those religions. Having prayed with Christians who have decided to renounce their involvement with yoga, I have no doubt that it is a practice which, for some people, can lead to a false passivity on the surface whilst masking a controlling demonic power over the emotions underneath.

Another example is mindfulness, which is being advocated in

schools and therapy centres for solving issues such as anxiety. This practice, also with roots in Buddhism, promotes a form of dissociation from the anxieties of the past or concerns for the future, by meditating on current thoughts and feelings whatever these might be. Without any rightful guarding on the mind, this practice can also make some vulnerable participants very open to a defiling spiritual influence, perhaps giving the appearance of calm but hiding an unintended door to the powers of darkness. Mindfulness is not the same as a search for truth and peace through the biblical process of getting right with God.

What about herbal treatment? God has given humankind an extraordinary variety of plants, some with properties that assist the body in the healing process, and for this we can be truly grateful. Rightly used, taking care of possible reactions with other medication, herbal treatment can be of benefit. However, we need to recognise that it is the application of the chemicals in the plants that God intended to bring us relief, not the transfer into our bodies of some hidden energy or power, as promoted in the practice of aromatherapy, for example. Examining the websites of several leading manufacturers of essential oils soon takes you to statements such as "aromatherapy brings attunement to the spirit" and "it's all about energy."

Homeopathy is not a herbal remedy. It's a treatment based on the belief that, by taking a sample from a plant that would normally cause the symptoms that are being treated, and massively diluting this sample, the supposed power absorbed during the dilution process will bring the cure desired from the resultant medication. The practice is occult, based on an unbiblical spiritual law that "like cures like". Putting faith in such a treatment is much more likely to cause spiritual oppression than to bring relief from depression.

I was reading an article recently about micro-dosing (using small doses) of psychedelic drugs such as LSD and mushrooms containing psilocybin, as a mood enhancer for those troubled by anxiety and depression. Interestingly, one person who is researching their possible use in tackling depression said, "One of the interesting things with psychedelics is that they work on something much deeper down." I suggest that they are unknowingly referring to the likely effect that hallucinogens can have on the integrity of the human spirit. Sadly, it will not be an effect that would come within the safe boundaries of God's way of spiritual restoration. I won't be recommending the use of magic mushrooms anytime soon!

[Recommended book: *The Dangers of Alternative Ways to Healing* by David Cross, ISBN 9781852405373]

Take some tips from Imogen!

I started this book with a testimony from *our friend Imogen*. As we near the end, here are some practical recommendations, many of which came from her. These suggestions significantly helped on her journey of healing with Jesus.

- Take little steps. They can still be strategic.
  Zechariah 4:10a… "For who has despised the day of small things?" NASB
- Make choices to slowly change habits which have become ingrained due to living in a state of depression. Every little step in agreement with God is honoured by Him

and reclaims ground from the enemy, making the next one easier.

- Get into nature, God's demonstration of His infinite creative ability.
- Make God your partner in a new kind of creative activity.
- Do something you really enjoy doing, or you think you would enjoy doing. From time to time, deliberately choose to do something different from your usual routine.
- Express your feelings: don't be afraid to shout them out in a safe place.
- Look after your body; it's God's property! Develop good habits for eating and sleeping.
- Counter isolation. It didn't help Elijah.
  1 Kings 19:10b…"I am the only one left – and now they are trying to kill me!" GNB
- Join something: a class, club, choir, and it doesn't have to be Christian.
- Counter self-pity. Serve others. Pray for others. Volunteer somewhere.
- Look for opportunities for laughter. It's probably the last thing a depressed person feels like doing but it is a God-given gift that has chemical and emotional benefits in the body. Find a book, a film or a TV programme that made you laugh in the past.
- Learn simple and practical ways of relaxing. For example, when an anxious moment occurs, find a comfortable position, and breathe in, counting to seven, and out, counting to eleven.
- Learn the warning signs for a bout of depression. The

earlier you notice it creeping in, the sooner you can take proactive steps.

- Consider getting a pet.

The power of proclaiming scripture

> *Psalm 119:160... The sum of Your word is truth, and every one of Your righteous ordinances is everlasting. NASB*

There is no doubt that a significant part of the journey out of depression is our recognition that we, as followers of Jesus, are engaged in a relentless spiritual battle. Of course, Jesus has utterly defeated the enemy at the Cross, but day by day we need to appropriate that victory into our own lives. We are encouraged to put on the full armour of God, so that we can stand firm against the schemes of the devil (Ephesians 6:11) and, not least, to take up the sword of the Spirit, which is the Word of God.

Under the anointing of the Holy Spirit, proclamation of Scripture can have a supernaturally powerful effect in pushing back the oppressive schemes of the evil one. Let the Lord direct you to the right Bible verses for your particular situation, but here are a few that may be helpful as a starting place for declaring dependence on the Lord and opposition to the deception of the enemy. Why not write them out and stick them around the house where they can be seen every day?

> *Psalm 42:11... Why are you in despair, O my soul? And why have you become disturbed within me? Hope in God, for I shall yet praise Him, The help of my countenance and my God. NASB*

Romans 5:5… And hope does not disappoint, because the love of God has been poured out within our hearts through the Holy Spirit who was given to us.

NASB

Deuteronomy 31:8… "The Lord is the one who goes ahead of you; He will be with you. He will not fail you or forsake you. Do not fear or be dismayed."

NASB

Psalm 34:18… The Lord is near to the brokenhearted and saves those who are crushed in spirit.

NASB

Job 33:28… 'He has redeemed my soul from going to the pit, and my life shall see the light.

NASB

Psalm 40:1-2… I waited patiently for the Lord; And He inclined to me and heard my cry. He brought me up out of the pit of destruction, out of the miry clay, And He set my feet upon a rock making my footsteps firm.

NASB

Isaiah 40:31… Yet those who wait for the Lord will gain new strength; they will mount up with wings like eagles, they will run and not get tired, they will walk and not become weary.

NASB

Key points from this chapter

- As we walk on the pathway of God's healing out of depression, there are some practical steps that we can take to aid that journey.

- Simple creativity, unrestricted by the pressure of performance, can be a very strategic opportunity to get in touch with the hidden distress of the heart.

- A balanced diet, incorporating foods known to be beneficial to mood, is an important support to the journey of healing

- Daily exercise in daylight has been proven to be very beneficial to those suffering with depression.

- A lifestyle of thankfulness has been shown to positively affect the chemical balances in the body, especially those associated with mood disorders.

- Stress and anxiety aggravate the symptoms of depression. Making choices to trust God at a deeper level, for provision and protection, will be an aid to de-stressing lives.

- Alternative holistic treatments are frequently advocated in order to alleviate anxiety and depression, but we need to be very careful. Any therapy seeking to alter our spiritual condition should be regarded as suspect if it ignores the teaching of Jesus, especially with regard to the issues of sin and God's forgiveness.

- We need to learn the warning signs that precede a bout of depression. The earlier we notice the depression creeping in, the sooner we can take proactive steps.

- The advice of those who have walked this journey of healing is worth noting. Here are some tips from those who have been mentioned in this book: take little steps, don't isolate, don't get into self-pity, get outside and take exercise, express the deep feelings, look after your body in regard to sleeping and eating, and look for opportunities to have a laugh.

- Proclaiming scripture powerfully restrains the voice of the enemy when he tries to discourage you.

CHAPTER 7

Final thoughts

Society is changing

The significant increase in the incidence of depression worldwide must have a cause. Either the biology of human beings is changing to make us more vulnerable to this disorder, or society is changing in such a way as to inflict more pressure on the human spirit, soul and body. I believe the latter is the truth. This is due to the breakdown in the traditional and biblical norms of family, gender, morality and human fulfilment, which is having a deeply oppressive effect on human life. In following Jesus Christ, we have an opportunity to reset our interaction with this created world, and to reset our priorities. We can pursue the fruit of His character rather than worldly success in work or finance. We can find fulfilment in a God-given destiny and know a confidence in His declaration of our true identity as one of His precious children.

Pursuit of fulfilment rather than happiness

We live in an age and a culture of entitlement, where the pursuit of happiness is seen as one of our foundational human rights. I read in a recent article, by a non-Christian writer, that such a quest is very likely to end in disappointment, if not depression. The author of the article had himself suffered with bouts of major depression, but he'd come to an important conclusion. When he made the switch in his life to prioritising a quest for fulfilment rather than happiness, the happiness came as a by-product and the depression became significantly less of a problem. Sadly, he had not yet discovered Jesus, the One who could fully answer his quest, but at least the principle was sound.

I believe that our greatest need, with regard to spiritual fulfilment, is to know deep down that we truly belong somewhere. No human pursuit can fully meet that need because there will always be a measure of uncertainty. But when, with absolute confidence, we experience the Spirit of God testifying with our human spirit that we are children of God (Romans 8:16), the quest is concluded, and the need is settled.

Finding both healing for the heart-damage of our lives and restoration from what has undermined confidence in our place in God's family, are strategic goals for followers of Jesus suffering from depression. The journey towards that goal will have challenging crossroads along the way but there is a destination of joy and hope. This cannot be stolen by the spiritual ruler of this troubled world, even in the inevitable ups and downs of life. Depression need no longer define our identity.

Being honest about depression

This book is not intended to imply that there is a quick fix for dealing with depression, but rather that the heart of God undoubtedly desires our restoration, and He will walk closely with us on that path of healing, however long it may be. Trusting Jesus and His promises in the Bible are the answer, for He alone has destroyed the works of the devil (1 John 3:8). Our task is simply to follow His instructions on the battlefield. While writing this book, I have sometimes shared my thoughts about this topic on Twitter©, and I received a heartfelt response from a person I will call Avril. She said, "I am very depressed right now, crying a lot, no motivation, bad thoughts, etc. But I know in my mind I've been here before and I will get out eventually. Sometimes it takes longer than others and sometimes it gets very bad. It's the truth of depression. But all of us are warriors!"

My prayer for Avril and all those struggling at this moment with this very painful and very dark disability is that our loving Heavenly Father would touch the place of despair inside and show each of you how to bring that place into the light. He wants to lead you into the place of assurance and hope, into the place of comfort and safety, and into the certainty of knowing that you are His child. You are precious members of His family and of enormous worth, with a unique destiny to be fulfilled in this lifetime.

By God's grace, this book is nearly complete

The idea of this book was initially sparked by hearing the testimonies of *our friends Iris and Deidre* some years ago while

I was on a visit to Ireland. When I was seeking the Lord as to whether to actually write the book, I had a remarkable experience while teaching on the topic in France. An intercessor, trusted by the church leaders where I was teaching, came up to me and said very strongly, through a translator, that God had just told her that I was to write down these truths and testimonies about depression. She went on to say that God had told her that He would help me from the very beginning to the very end.

Nothing quite like that has ever happened to me before, or since. However, I can honestly say that I have known the Lord's clear leading from the first moment I began to type the words of this book. The primary purpose has always been to encourage every follower of Jesus who is wrestling with this issue to believe that God truly has a way through to wholeness and freedom. I am not pretending it will be easy, but I know that embarking on the journey with Him will not end in disappointment. May I encourage you to make a start today, if you haven't already done so, by asking Him to shine His light into every area of darkness from the past that has a bearing on this painful disorder today.

Jesus is the antidote to hopelessness

Hopelessness is one of the most common symptoms of depression. A damaged human spirit finds it hard not only to embrace the fulness of a God-given destiny in this life, but also to be assured of the certainty of our eternal inheritance. A friend of mine recently said that, for a follower of Jesus, hope is not something we can manufacture but it is like a reservoir stored in heaven which we can tap into anytime, by the enabling of the Holy Spirit.

> *Colossians 1:5a... Because of the hope laid up for you in heaven, of which you previously heard in the word of truth.*
>
> NASB

Our friend Agnes admitted in her testimony that she still has "wobbles" in her moods. Don't be troubled or feel condemned when this happens to you. Just admit the reality of the way you feel and reach out for the Lord's touch. Learn to recognise the signs and, with His help, take some of the prayerful and practical steps we have been considering. He is ready:

> *Deuteronomy 33:26-27... "There is no one like the God of Israel. He rides across the heavens to help you, across the skies in majestic splendour. The eternal God is your refuge, and his everlasting arms are under you. He drives out the enemy before you; he cries out, 'Destroy them!'"*
>
> NLT

Giving God the last word

My wife Denise and I were recently teaching on the topic of depression back in Ireland. Just before we left home, we had a message from one of the faithful intercessors who pray for the work of Ellel Ministries. She knew that this teaching was to be taking place over the next few days and had been waiting on the Lord for what He might want to say. She felt sure that He wanted to highlight Psalm 23, and to say that He is always there even through the times of the deepest darkness. Here is the Psalm from the Good News Bible. May the Lord clearly speak His comfort to your spirit through these well-known words:

The Lord is my shepherd;
I have everything I need,
He lets me rest in fields of green grass and leads me to quiet pools of fresh water.
He gives me new strength.
He guides me in the right paths, as he has promised.
Even if I go through the deepest darkness, I will not be afraid, Lord, for you are with me.
Your shepherd's rod and staff protect me.
You prepare a banquet for me, where all my enemies can see me;
You welcome me as an honoured guest and fill my cup to the brim.
I know that your goodness and love will be with me all my life;
And your house will be my home as long as I live.

David Cross

David Cross is Regional Director for Ellel Ministries in Western Europe.

He graduated from Nottingham University in 1969 and qualified as a chartered civil engineer, leading to a varied working career, which included building roads and bridges in the Highlands of Scotland and, in the early 1980's, overseeing the construction of new town development in the New Territories area of Hong Kong. It was here that a huge personal change of direction occurred when he gave his life to Jesus.

Returning to Scotland, David became very active in church life and in leading ski tours in the Cairngorm Mountains. In order to further the Christian healing ministry in the Highlands, as an elder in the Church of Scotland, he and others in the local church made contact with Ellel Ministries in 1991, and two years later David and his wife Denise joined the Ministry at the international headquarters of Ellel Grange, near Lancaster.

David and Denise have three children and eight grandchildren, all giving much joy in the midst of very busy lives. Besides the thrill of sharing God's truth through teaching and writing, David loves walking and photography. His authoritative explanation of God's word has brought understanding and healing to many who have been confused and damaged by the ungodly ideologies of today's world.

David has written seven other books: *Soul-Ties*, *God's Covering*, *Trapped by Control*, *The Dangers of Alternative Ways of Healing* (with John Berry), *the A-Z Guide to the Healing Ministry*, *What's Wrong with Human Rights?*, *Tweet-sized thoughts on God-sized issues and God's Way out of Depression*.

Ellel Ministries
International

Our Vision

Ellel Ministries is a non-denominational Christian Mission Organization with a vision to resource and equip the Church by welcoming people, teaching them about the Kingdom of God and healing those in need (Luke 9:11).

Our Mission

Our mission is to fulfil the above vision throughout the world, as God opens the doors, in accordance with the Great Commission of Jesus and the calling of the Church to proclaim the Kingdom of God by preaching the good news, healing the broken-hearted and setting the captives free. We are, therefore, committed to evangelism, healing, deliverance, discipleship and training. The particular scriptures on which our mission is founded are Isaiah 61:1–7; Matthew 28:18–20; Luke 9:1–2; 9:11; Ephesians 4:12; 2 Timothy 2:2.

Our Basis of Faith

God is a Trinity. God the Father loves all people. God the Son, Jesus Christ, is Saviour and Healer, Lord and King. God the Holy Spirit indwells Christians and imparts the dynamic power by which they are enabled to continue Christ's ministry. The Bible is the divinely inspired authority in matters of faith, doctrine and conduct, and is the basis for teaching.

For details about the current worldwide activities of Ellel Ministries International please go to: www.ellel.org

Ellel Ministries International
Ellel Grange
Ellel
Lancaster, LA2 0HN
United Kingdom
Tel (+44) (0)1524 751 651

Other titles in the Truth & Freedom Series

All available in eBook format from all the major eBook readers

Anger
How do you handle it?
Paul & Liz Griffin

Size: 5.5"x8.5"
Pages: 112
ISBN: 9781852404505

Hope & Healing for the Abused
Paul & Liz Griffin

Size: 5.5"x8.5"
Pages: 128
ISBN: 9781852404802

Intercession & Healing
Breaking through with God
Fiona Horrobin

Size: 5.5"x8.5"
Pages: 176
ISBN: 9781852405007

Soul Ties
The unseen bond in relationships
David Cross

Size: 5.5"x8.5"
Pages: 128
ISBN: 9781852404512

God's Covering
A place of healing
David Cross

Size: 5.5"x8.5"
Pages: 192
ISBN: 9781852404857

The Dangers of Alternative Ways to Healing
How to avoid new age deceptions
David Cross & John Berry

Size: 5.5"x8.5"
Pages: 176
ISBN: 9781852405373

Trapped by Control
How to find freedom
David Cross

Size: 5.5"x8.5"
Pages: 112
ISBN: 9781852405014

Rescue from Rejection
Finding Security
in God's Loving
Acceptance
Denise Cross

Size: 5.5"x8.5"
Pages: 160
ISBN: 9781852405380

Healing from the consequences of Accident, Shock and Trauma
Peter Horrobin

Size: 5.5"x8.5"
Pages: 168
ISBN: 9781852407438

Stepping Stones to the Father Heart of God
Margaret Silvester

Size: 5.5" x 8.5"
Pages: 176
ISBN: 9781852406233

www.sovereignworld.com